Lanascapes of
CYPRUS

a countryside guide

Geoff Daniel

Fourth edition
Revised by John and Christine Oldfield

SUNFLOWER BOOKS

Fourth edition
Copyright © 2004
Sunflower Books™
12 Kendrick Mews
London SW7 3HG, UK

ISBN 1-85691-229-9

In the Troodos Mountains

Important note to the reader

We have tried to ensure that the descriptions and maps in this book are error-free at press date. Travellers to Cyprus will be aware of recent changes in the naming of major towns and cities, such as Lefkosia for Nicosia, and Lemesos for Limassol. This is part of official moves to create a stronger national identity in the Greek part of the island. We have incorporated the major changes, but you may encounter others. This book will be updated, where necessary, whenever future printings permit. It will be very helpful for us to receive your comments (sent in care of the publishers, please) for the updating of future printings.

We also rely on those who use this book — especially walkers — to take along a good supply of common sense when they explore. Conditions change fairly rapidly on Cyprus, and ***storm damage or bulldozing may make a route unsafe at any time***. If the route is not as we outline it here, and your way ahead is not secure, return to the point of departure. ***Never attempt to complete a tour or walk under hazardous conditions!*** Please read carefully the notes on pages 19 and 41 to 48, as well as the introductory comments at the beginning of each tour and walk (regarding road conditions, equipment, grade, distances and time, etc). Explore **safely**, while at the same time respecting the beauty of the countryside.

Cover photograph: in the Avagas Gorge (Walk 16)
Title page: Mount Adelphi signpost

Fieldwork for this edition by John and Christine Oldfield
Photographs: 17, 20-21, 25 (top left), 29 (bottom right), 30, 53, 59
  (right), 66 (right), 78, 85 (top), 92-93, 95 (bottom), 106-107, 113: John
  and Christine Oldfield; all other photographs by the author
Maps and plans: John Underwood
Drawings: Katharina Kelly
A CIP catalogue record for this book is available from the British Library.
Printed and bound in Spain: A G Elkar, 48180 Loiu

10 9 8 7 6 5 4 3 2 1

Contents

Lachi harbour

❀ Preface _____

Cyprus, birthplace of the mythical love goddess Aphrodite, yields its greatest pleasures to the visitor who makes an effort towards closer acquaintance.

If you are content with sun, sand, surf and soured brandy, then you won't be disappointed. But deeper exploration of this special island, on foot or on wheels, coupled with a healthy curiosity about its people and its traditions, will reward you with experiences to treasure for a lifetime. Should your first visit to Cyprus be the start of an incurable love affair, do not be at all surprised!

This Fourth edition of *Landscapes of Cyprus* is divided into three main sections, each with its own introduction.

For **motorists**, there are car tours taking in lively resorts, picturesque villages, mountain spectacle, fast new roads and very slow old ones. There are suggestions for 4WD enthusiasts too.

Picnickers can take their choice of authorised sites with benches and barbecue facilities, or out-of-the-way locations along the course of a walk.

Walkers have a comprehensive guide to Cyprus on foot, totally revised and updated. The walks cover most areas of the island, most are within the stride of anyone sound in wind and limb, and most are easily accessible.

Cyprus — past
The turbulent history of Cyprus dates back to the Stone Age, and the island has undergone numerous changes of 'ownership' over the centuries. Turks, Romans, Greeks, Venetians, and the British have all played a part in the island's destiny. In Lefkosia the Cyprus Museum and the Museum of National Struggle are well worth visiting to gain an appreciation of the past.

Throughout the island, richly historic sites beckon the curious traveller, not least the imposing 13th-century castle at Kolossi, Lefkosia's Venetian walls, the ancient Tombs of the Kings at Pafos, and the Neolithic settlement at Khirokitia.

In the mountainous Troodos region, nine churches on UNESCO's World Heritage list are rightly famous for beautiful frescoes painted between the 11th and 15th centuries.

Cyprus — present

Since 1960 Cyprus has been an independent republic within the British Commonwealth. In 1974 Turkey occupied the north and northeastern regions, physically dividing the island and establishing a state which remains unrecognised in the international community. It is not possible to travel freely between the two sectors except for a 24-hour period (through the Ledra checkpoint in Lefkosia). *Landscapes of Cyprus* therefore regrettably confines its coverage to the south. A future edition might incorporate the Turkish-controlled area, if the political situation changes.

Cyprus — people

For all their upheavals, Greek Cypriots remain among the most cheerful, gregarious and hospitable folk you could ever meet. English is widely understood, but even a stumbling attempt at a few words of Greek (see page 47) on the part of the visitor is warmly appreciated. Cypriot hospitality is legendary — *kopiaste!* (come in and join us!) — and should always be accepted, even if sparingly.

Cyprus — environment

Walking, and other leisure activities which respect the island's somewhat fragile environment, will become increasingly important as conventional coast-based tourism heads towards saturation point. The creation of a national park in the beautiful Akamas region in the west is a positive move to ensure protection of sensitive areas such as the green turtle nesting grounds at Lara Beach.

Acknowledgements

I am indebted to the following:

For fieldwork on this updated and expanded Fourth edition: John and Christine Oldfield, authors of the Sunflower guides to the Costa Blanca and Andalucia.

For maps and plans: the Department of Lands and Surveys, Lefkosia.

For practical assistance and suggestions: Lillian Panayi, Tourism Officer of the Cyprus Tourism Organisation, London; David Pearlman and Jan Horton of ExAlt Travel, Pafos; Yiannis Christofides, the Hotel Minerva, Platres; Adrian Akers-Douglas of the Laona Project

Books

It must be emphasised that *Landscapes of Cyprus* is a guide to countryside exploration and intended to be used in addition to a standard guide, of which there are many. Christos Georgiades' *Nature of Cyprus — environment, flora and fauna*, available on the island, is a valuable pictorial reference work; Colin Thubron's *Journey into Cyprus*, an account of a pre-1974 walk round the island, is a scholarly but absorbing read; and Lawrence Durrell's classic, *Bitter Lemons*, is an amusing and poignant portrait of a Cyprus long gone.

❀ Getting about

A **hired car** is undoubtedly the most practical way of exploring Cyprus. Numerous companies offer a wide range of vehicles, from runabouts to prestige models. Small 4WD soft-tops are increasingly popular, and their modest extra cost is worth considering if you plan trips into mountains or remote regions — such is the rough condition of many minor road surfaces. I have included some 4WD route suggestions in this book.

Coach tours operate from the main tourist centres, and offer a painless introduction to road conditions and a comfortable view of island scenery.

Intercity buses are an inexpensive way of moving from one place to another, perhaps for tackling a walk out of a different centre from your hotel base.

Taxis operate in profusion in the towns, more sparsely in villages, and all are identified by a prefix 'T' to the registration number. Rates are fixed by the authorities, and urban taxis are obliged to operate a meter on all journeys. Fares are not high, but on longer journeys it is wise to agree a price in advance. In town you will likely ride in a new Mercedes, but in a village it will probably be something older and more interesting!

Service taxis are a useful way of getting from town to town if you're not in a hurry. They ply between major centres approximately every half-hour and will pick you up at your hotel and take you anywhere central at your destination, picking up and dropping off other passengers en route. They are useful on walks which end on a service taxi route: simply ask a bar or café owner to request a service taxi stop on its next run. Rates are very cheap for the service offered. You will share your journey with other passengers (possibly in a minibus), but this is the only inconvenience.

Local buses are not very helpful for the walker; essentially they bring village folk to town in early morning and take them home later in the day.

Service taxi and bus timetables are given on pages 121-133, but *do* collect an up-to-date timetable (including fare details) and taxi operator list from any tourist office as soon as you arrive on Cyprus, and check also the availability of any extra seasonal services.

LEFKOSIA (Nicosia)

1 Arts and crafts centre
2 Tourist information
3 Post office
4 Municipal library
5 Town hall
6 Museum of the National Struggle
7 Folk art museum
8 Archbishop's palace and Makarios Cultural Centre
9 Municipal cultural centre
10 Police station
11 Cyprus Museum
12 Telephones
13 Municipal theatre
14 House of Representatives
15 Hospital
16 UK high commission
17 Cyprus Airways
18 US embassy
19 Museum (contemporary art)
20 Stadium
21 German embassy
Cyprus Interurban Taxi Co Ltd (service taxis)
1 Intercity Buses Co, Nea Amorza, Alepa Bus Co, 'Solis' Minibus
2 Platres Bus
3 Clarios Bus Co, EMAN
4 PEAL

Barbaro

Quirini

Loredano

Flatro

LEOPHOROS KYRINIAS

KHRISTODHOULOU

ARASTA

ERMOU

KAPOTA **E**

ERMOU

ERMOU

PHOU

LEDRAS

TRIKUPPI

VARNAVA

6

7

8

Caraffa

SPYRO

9

K.TENA

GRIGORIOU

ALEXANDHRIAS

LEOPHOROS SALAMINOS

Podocataro

F

Platia
Solomou

1

2

2 **1**

5 **3**

4 D'Avila

3
Costanza

LEOPHOROS STASINOU

4

THEODHOTOU

RQU I

LEOPHOROS ARKHIEPISKOPOU

DHIYENI AKRITA

KALLIPOLEOS

17

SANTA ROZA

MAKARIOU III

N

0   0.5 km

18

LEOPHOROS KENNEDY

A

PAFOS
(Paphos)

1   Tourist information
2   Cyprus Airways
3   Market
4   Police station
5   Stadium
6   Library
7   Hospital
8   Town hall
9   Telephones
10 Bishop's palace
11 Cathedral
12 Ethnological museum
13 Post office
14 Underground church
15 Theatre
16 Roman theatre
17 Latin cathedral (ruin)
18 Frankish baths
19 House of Dionysos
20 Byzantine fortress
21 St Paul's Pillar
22 Post office
23 Customs house
24 Pafos castle
25 Medieval fort (ruin)
26 Central parking
🚐 Cyprus Interurban Taxi Co
     (service taxis)
🚌1 Nea Amorza
🚌2 Alepa Bus Co

LARNAKA
(Larnaca)

1 Tourist information
2 Post office
3 Law courts
4 Police station
5 St Joseph's convent
6 Archaeological museum
7 Acropolis of Kition
8 Tennis courts
9 Phoenician temple
10 Mycenean walls
11 Market
12 Mycenean site
13 Hospital
14 Customs house
15 Park and zoo
16 Library
17 Telephones
18 Stadium
19 Central market
20 Cultural centre
21 Medieval fort (museum)
22 Phaneromeni
23 St Lazarus

🚕 Cyprus Interurban Taxi Co (service taxis)
🚌 1 Intercity Buses Co, EMAN
🚌 2 PEAL Bus Co
🚌 3 Larnaka Buses Ltd (Ayios Lazaros Square)

LEMESOS (Limassol)

1 Tourist information
2 Castle and museum
3 Town hall
4 Bishop's seat
5 Market
6 Telephones
7 Administration offices
8 Police headquarters
9 Hospital
10 Library
11 Stadium
12 Zoo and public gardens
13 Theatre
14 Archaeological museum
15 Distillery
🚐 Cyprus Interurban Taxi Co (service taxis)
🚌1 Intercity Buses Co, Nea Amorza, Alepa Bus
🚌2 Travel Express
🚌3 Agros Bus
🚌4 EAL

AYIA (Agia) NAPA

1 Tourist information & Cyprus Airways
2 Post office
3 Telephones
4 Monastery
5 Sefebis Square
6 Bus station (EMAN)

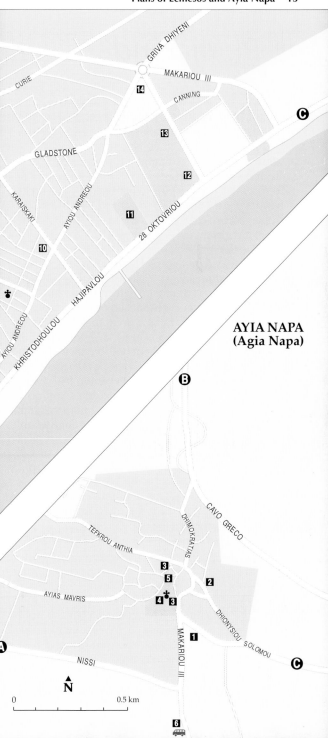

GRIVA DHIYENI

MAKARIOU III

CURIE

CANNING

14

C

13

GLADSTONE

12

KARAISKAKI

AYIOU ANDREOU

11

28 OKTOVRIOU

10

AYIOU ANDREOU

HAJIPAVLOU

KHRISTODHOULOU

AYIA NAPA
(Agia Napa)

B

CAVO GRECO

TEFKROU ANTHIA

DHIMOKRATIAS

3

5

2

AYIAS MAVRIS

4 **3**

A

DHIONYSIOU SOLOMOU

1

MAKARIOU III

NISSI

C

N

0   0.5 km

6

● Picnicking

Picnicking is great fun on Cyprus, not least for Cypriots themselves, who will happily tuck into an outdoor feast, especially at weekends or on festival days. This enthusiasm does not extend to walking for pleasure, however, so you are most likely to come across groups of local families enjoying an outing at an official site which is easily accessible by car.

Such a site might suit your requirements — or you may prefer to seek out somewhere much more secluded along the route of a walk. Much of the island is open countryside, but it is a matter of common sense and courtesy not to picnic within any obvious fencing or boundary.

Official sites: The Cyprus Tourism Organisation and Forestry Department have established about 30 sites. Most of them are concentrated in the Troodos mountain region, but there is an excellent site near Polis, north of Pafos, close to several walks and car tours described in this book. The best sites offer car parking, toilet facilities, drinking water, tables and benches, barbecue facilities and play areas for children. At some of the smaller sites in less visited areas, facilities might be minimal. Official sites are indicated in the car touring notes and on the fold-out touring map by the symbol (🛆). Remember that in winter and early spring many will be inaccessible, since they lie along rough mountain roads. A leaflet describing all these sites and a few official camp sites (the only places where camping is allowed) is available from tourist information centres on the island.

Alternative suggestions: If you prefer a picnic 'away from it all', or if you find official sites crowded (likely at weekends and in high summer), you could picnic along one of the walks in this book.

All the information you need to get to one of these 'private' picnics is given on the following pages, *where picnic numbers correspond to walk numbers*, so that you can quickly find the general location by looking at the pull-out touring map (on which the area of each walk is shown in green within a white circle). I include transport details (🚌: how to get there by bus; 🚗: where to park if you come by car or taxi), how long a walk you'll have *each way*, and views or setting. Beside the picnic title

14

you'll find a map reference: the exact location of the picnic spot is shown on this *walking* map by the symbol *P*. Finally, to help you choose the right setting, many of the picnic spots are illustrated.

Please remember that these 'alternative' picnic places are generally off the beaten track: you will need to wear sensible shoes and almost certainly a sunhat (the symbol ○ at the right of a picnic title indicates a *picnic place in full sun*).

If travelling to your picnic by service taxi or bus, please be sure to collect an up-to-date transport time-table, with operators' telephone numbers.

If travelling to your picnic by hired car, watch out for animals and children on country roads and drive especially carefully through narrow village streets. Do park well off the road — without damaging plants — and *never* block a road or track.

All picnickers should read the country code on page 19 and go quietly in the countryside.

1 MOUNT OLYMPUS (map pages 54-55, Troodos photographs on pages 51 and 56)

by car: 45min on foot   *by bus and taxi: 45min on foot*
🚗: park on Troodos main street (8km north of Platres).
🚌: take a bus (but check if there is a suitable return!) or taxi from Lemesos to Platres, then go on to Troodos by local taxi.
From Troodos, follow Walk 1 along the Atalante trail for the first 3km, to an open area where there are numerous picnicking possibilities in pleasant surroundings and with extensive views. On the Artemis trail (the Alternative walk) there are also plenty of benches with stunning views where picnics can be enjoyed.

2 MAKRYA KONTARKA (map pages 54-55, photograph page 56)

by car: 15-45min on foot   *by bus and taxi: 15-45min on foot*
🚗 and 🚌: as Picnic 1 above
From Troodos, take the nature trail from the southern end of the main street as described in Walk 2 for 15 minutes, to the group of benches among tall pines shown on page 56. This is a cool spot, but a picnic at the end of the trail (Makrya Kontarka; 45min), with magnificent views, is highly recommended, although there is little shade.

3 CALEDONIAN FALLS (map pages 54-55, photograph page 53)

by car: 5-45min on foot   *by bus: not practical*
🚗: park near the Caledonian Falls nature trail, by the side of a rough road that leads from a point slightly west of the trout farm (see map for car symbol). From here it's a five minute walk to the falls (signposted). Alternatively, park at the start of the nature trail (see Walk 3, page 53) and follow the walk to the falls, or find a suitable place to sit beside the Kryos River within a shorter distance.
Shady trees and pleasant ferns characterise this picnic spot.

4 MESAPOTAMOS (map pages 54-55, photograph page 57)

by car: up to 10min on foot   *by bus and taxi: up to 10min on foot*
🚗: park at Mesapotamos Monastery: rough roads lead from Platres or
Saittas to this disused retreat.
🚌: take a bus (see Picnic 1) from Lemesos to Platres, then go on by
local taxi (be sure to arrange your return).
*This is a wooded setting with good shade. There are two official sites
nearby, but there's also scope for quieter outings.*

5 ABOVE PSILON DHENDRON (map pages 54-55)

by car or taxi: 6min on foot   *by bus and taxi: 30min on foot*
🚗 to Psilon Dhendron or 🚌 to Platres (see Picnic 1) and walk uphill
to Psilon Dhendron
*Follow Walk 5 for 6min, to a bench set on a rise to your right. There
are lovely views down to Platres and the trout farm and up to the
mountains; ample shade.*

7 MADHARI RIDGE (map pages 62-63, photograph page 63)

by car: 15-40min on foot   *by bus: not practical*
🚗: park near the start of the nature trail described in Walk 7.
*From the nature trail information board, climb to the bench at the
15min-point for a short walk offering superb views over Kyperounda
village; or follow Walk 7 for about 40 minutes, to the clearing with
views over the Mesaoria Plain and towards Mount Adelphi.*

8 PERA PEDI (map page 64)

by car: just 1min on foot   *by bus: not practical*
🚗: park in Pera Pedi
*Follow Walk 8 to the Kryos River; a lovely peaceful area has been
created, with benches, plenty of shade and the sound of running water.*

10 MOUNT TRIPYLOS (map page 69, nearby photograph page 70)

by car: 40min on foot   *by bus: not accessible*
🚗: park at the Dhodheka Anemi junction (the 55km-point in Car tour
3, page 28), or see Walk 10, page 69.
*Look for the gated track (from which vehicles are barred) on the right,
signposted to Mount Tripylos, and follow it for 2km to the peak (1362m/
4470ft), from where there are magnificent views; also a fire-watch
station and a small picnic area in a lovely setting.*

12 KATHIKAS SPRING (map page 73, photograph page 25)

by car: 20min on foot   *by bus: not practical*
🚗: park at Kathikas (the 27km-point in Car tour 1).
*Follow Walk 12 to the 20min-point. This is a tranquil setting with a
shady bench and a spring (operate the pump by a handle on the right).*

13 MAVROKOLYMBOS DAM (map and nearby photograph page 75)

by car: up to 15min on foot   *by bus: not practical*
🚗: park near the dam, on the Akoursos road (signposted off the main
Pafos-Coral Bay road).
You'll find ample quiet spots on the banks of this irrigation reservoir.

14 LARA BEACH (map and photographs pages 78-79) ○

by car or boat: up to 10min on foot   *by bus: not accessible*
🚗: park at Lara Beach or take a ⛴ from Pafos (see Walk 14, page 76).
A quiet undeveloped beach with a single, seasonal restaurant

Picnic 20: benches 35 minutes up the 'Aphrodonis' trail

18a ALEKHTORA VALLEY VIEWS (map page 88) ○

by car: 34min on foot   *by bus: not practical*
🚐: park well off the road near the 'Alekhtora' sign and fruit packing factory at the start of Walk 18 (page 86).
Follow Walk 18 to the 34min-point. Go up on to the antenna platform and walk 50m past the antenna. Choose a spot on the right —sitting on the grass or the rocks — overlooking the valley. No shade.

18b KHAPOTAMI GORGE OVERLOOK (map page 88) ○

by car: up to 1h08min on foot   *by bus: not practical*
🚐: park as for Picnic 18a above.
Follow Walk 18 to the 1h08min-point, at the edge of the rocky terracing. As long as you don't mind dodging the goat droppings, this is a spectacular site. No shade.

20 'APHRODONIS' TRAIL (map on reverse of touring map, photographs above and page 95)

by car, or by bus and taxi: up to 1h10min on foot
🚐: park at the tourist pavilion at the Baths of Aphrodite.
🚌 from Pafos to Polis; then bus (summer only) or taxi to the Baths
There are numerous lovely spots on the first, shared part of the two trails; the benches at trail point 11 (35min) are ideal, as is the shady hollow by Pyrgos tis Rigaenas (1h10min).

21 SMIYIES (map on reverse of touring map)

by car: no walking, or up to about 2h on foot   *by bus: not practical*
🚐: park at the picnic site; the rough road is motorable in a standard car in dry weather. Or park in Neokhorio and walk (50min each way).
A well-sited picnic area, with water, tables and benches; several short walk opportunities in the immediate vicinity (see page 94 and map).

22 DROUSSEIA (map page 96) ○

by car: 20min on foot   *by bus: not practical*
🚐: park behind the hotel in Drousseia (see *Alternative walk, page 96*)
Follow Alternative walk 22 to the 20min-point. A narrow path leads to the giant rocks. There is little shade, but fantastic views across to the Troodos, Mount Olympus, Polis Bay and the north coast.

23 MILIOU (map page 99) ○

by car: 25min uphill on foot	*by bus: not practical*

🚗: park as for Walk 23 (page 98)
Follow the Short walk to the junction at the 25min-point. Sit on rocks near the track junction, with panoramic views. No shade.

25a FISHERMAN'S TRAIL (map and photograph pages 104-105)

by car: 2-10min on foot	*by bus: not practical*

🚗: park at the signposted nature trail (see Short walk, page 103)
Picnic spots abound on this nature trail — at the water's edge (limited shade) or at the hilltop shelter (shade, benches, fine views)

25b A VIEW FOR THE GODS (map and photograph pages 104-105)

by car: 1h04min uphill on foot	*by bus: not accessible*

🚗: park as for Alternative walk 1 on page 103
Follow Walk 25 from the 31min-point to the 4-way junction at the 1h18min-point. Take the track straight ahead, up to a hexagonal shelter. Views in all directions give you a matchless panorama — from Mount Olympus in the north to the Yermasoyia Dam in the south, Kouklia in the west and the mountains above Larnaka in the east. Benches to sit on, shade.

27 STAVROVOUNI (map page 110, photos pages 37 and 111) ○

by car: 5min on foot	*by bus: not practical*

🚗: park just below the monastery.
From the top of this striking pedestal you have a panoramic view of Cyprus. Women are not allowed in the monastery, but views from the car park are equally impressive. Toilets; sometimes a fruit stall.

28 NEAR KITI TOWER (map page 112, nearby photo page 113) ○

by car: 56min on foot (or 8min if you drive as far as the watchtower)	
by bus: 56min on foot	

🚗 or 🚌 to Kiti
Follow Walk 28 to the 56min-point and pick your spot on this quiet, pebbly beach. Limited shade, lots of salty water!

29 EAST OF AYIA NAPA (map pages 116-117, photographs pages 40 and 118) ○

by car: 5-40min on foot	*by bus: 15-40min on foot*

🚗: park at Ayia Napa near the start of Walk 29 (see page 115).
🚌: check Ayia Napa region times and routes at a tourist office.
The early stages of Walk 29 offer numerous picnic opportunities, the best sand being at Kermia Beach (no shade). Head straight there by car if you do not wish to walk.

30 AYII SARANTA (map map pages 116-117, photograph page 120)

by car: 20min on foot	*by bus: not practical*

🚗: park short of the transmitter tower, then walk round to Ayii Saranta, as described in Short walk 30 on page 119.
A pleasant location in the shadow of the unusual little church shown on page 120, set on a hill in the quiet agricultural area inland from the lively resort of Ayia Napa.

A country code for walkers and motorists

The experienced rambler is accustomed to following a 'country code' on his walks, but the tourist out for a lark can unwittingly cause damage, harm animals and even endanger his own life. A code for behaviour based on self-discipline is important wherever people are free to roam over the countryside, and doubly so on rugged terrain. On Cyprus, special care should be taken to avoid fires.

- **Do not light fires**, except in the areas provided at official picnic sites. Never allow children to play with matches. Never throw cigarette ends away in the forest. If you see a fire in or near a forest, put it out if you can. If you cannot, use the nearest telephone (T on our maps) to inform the police or Forestry Department.
- **Do not frighten animals**. By making loud noises or trying to touch or photograph them, you may cause them to run in fear and be hurt.
- **Leave all gates just as you found them**. Although animals may not be in evidence, the gates do have a purpose; generally they keep grazing or herded sheep or goats in — or out of — an area.
- **Protect all wild and cultivated plants**. Leave them in place for others to enjoy. Flowers will die before you get them back to your hotel; fruit is obviously someone's livelihood. *Never walk over cultivated ground.*
- **Take all your litter away with you**.
- **Do not block roads or tracks**. Park where you will not inconvenience anyone or cause danger.
- **Walkers: *do not take risks!*** Don't attempt walks beyond your capacity. Remember that there is very little twilight on Cyprus … nor are there any officially-organised rescue services. If you were to injure yourself, it might be a very long time before you are found. **Do *not* walk alone**, and *always* tell a responsible person exactly where you are going and what time you plan to return. On any but a very short walk near to villages, be sure to carry a compass, whistle, torch, an extra woollie and plenty of water and high-energy food like chocolate.

Wild pigs are a rare sight — even more so than the elusive moufflon

❀ Touring

Driving on the roads of Cyprus (keep to the left) can be a great pleasure, but it does at times call for the ability to resist impatience. It can also be tiring in the hot sun. So do not aim for long distances. Better to really *enjoy* a shorter run than simply clock up kilometres. Punctuate days out in the car with short walks and relaxing picnics.

My touring notes are brief: they include little history or information that can be gleaned from standard guides or leaflets available free at all tourist centres and pavilions. Instead, I concentrate on the logistics of touring: road conditions, viewpoints, distances, and good places to rest. Most of all, I emphasise possibilities for **walking** and **picnicking** (the symbol *P* alerts you to a picnic spot; see pages 14-18). While some of the walk suggestions may not be suitable for a long car tour, you may discover a landscape you would like to explore at leisure another day.

The tours (which include 4WD suggestions — hiring a jeep is highly recommended) radiate from the three

main tourist centres: Pafos, Lemesos and Larnaka. Bearing in mind that Cyprus is the third largest island in the Mediterranean — some 222 kilometres (138 miles) from east to west — do not plan to tour the *entire* island without an overnight stop or two!

The large touring map is designed to be held out opposite the touring notes and contains all the information you will need outside the towns (town plans with exit routes keyed to the touring map are on pages 8 to 13).

Make sure your **car is in good condition**: keep a regular check on tyres, brakes, water, oil and lights. Always carry warm clothing (especially in the mountains, even in summer) in case of delays or breakdowns. Allow plenty of time for **stops**: my times include only short breaks at viewpoints labelled (📷) in the touring notes. **Telephones** (in green kiosks) are located in towns and most villages, near post offices, but most bars and cafes will allow you to make a local call if necessary. **WC**s are available in larger centres; others are found in bars and cafes. **Distances** quoted are *cumulative* kilometres from the starting point. A key to the **symbols** in the notes is on the touring map.

All motorists should read the country code on page 19 and respect the environment.

While it's a good idea to tour the island in a jeep and bounce with ease along tracks to places like Cedar Valley, Lara Beach and the Makheras Forest, you can still reach most of the walks in this book in a standard hire car. While you would need a jeep to get to the start of Walk 26 at the Kionia picnic site below Mount Makheras, if you are only going to visit the monastery there is now a good asphalted route via Odou, Pharmakas, Ghourri and Lazania. This is a beautiful drive, as you can see in this photograph of the tomato fields above Odou.

1 WESTERN WAYS

Pafos • Coral Bay • Peyia • Kathikas • Drousseia • Prodhromi • Lachi • Baths of Aphrodite • (4WD options) • Polis • Skoulli • Stroumbi • Pafos

115km/71mi; about 3h30min driving; leave Pafos on the road to the Tomb of the Kings (Exit D)

On route: ⊟ at Smiyies (4WD Route A); Picnics (see pages 14-18) 12, 13, 20, 22, (23); also 14 (4WD routes); Walks (11), 12, 13, 15, 19-22, (23); also 14, 16 (4WD routes)

A leisurely full-day tour on good roads which are narrow and twisting in places. If you've hired a jeep for the first time, either of the suggestions on page 24 offers a good introduction to the joys of rough-track driving! Both 4WD routes make shorter circuits than the full car tour — about 80km in each case.

Leave Pafos on the road to the Tomb of the Kings (Exit D), at the traffic light junction between Pafos and Nea Pafos, just north of the Apollo Hotel. At 13km pass a sign-posted turning to the right — a rough track to Mavro-kolymbos Dam (*P*13); it's on the route of Walk 13 from Kissonerga. At 14km reach **Coral Bay★** (▲▲✕🎦), the popular beach and resort area shown on page 75, where Walk 13 ends. If you need petrol, head about 1km or so towards Ayios Yeoryios, where you will find a station (🚭) on the right... and behind it, a reptile display centre.

From Coral Bay, head inland to **Peyia** (18km ✚✕🎦), a large, cheerful, non-touristy village set on a hillside. As you climb beyond it, the views (🎦) over the coast become at first appealing and then magnificent as you head for **Kathikas** (27km; *P*12), which means 'perched on a hill'. Walk 12 sets off from the Laona Project Visitors' Centre here, and if you find it open, be sure to obtain the excellent booklet, *Discover Laona*. The Laona Project is a laudable attempt to breathe economic life back into some of the old villages of western Cyprus, while retaining their cultural and social identity.

Through Kathikas, there's an option to cross the main road and detour a few kilometres to Pano and Kato Akourdhalia, two small Laona villages (combined population 100!) noted for springtime almond blossom, a herb garden, folk museum, excellent taverna/guest-house project, and the 12th-century church of Ayia Paraskevi.

Our route bears left at the main road for a few minutes, then turns left at a signpost through **Pano** and **Kato Arodhes** (32km), **Inia** (34km) and the larger village of **Drousseia** (36km ▲▲✕🎦*P*22; Walk 15 and Alternative walk 22), with its splendid views round the compass on a clear day. Return to the main road, and turn left to

View down to the Baths of Aphrodite from the end of the Adonis trail (Walk 20)

continue the tour — or first turn right briefly, then left, at a signpost to Kritou Terra, from where there is a short and very pretty walk to Terra and back (Walk 22; photographs page 97).

Continuing north from Drousseia on the main route, come to the coast road at **Prodhromi** and turn left to reach the fishing harbour and resort area of **Lachi** (50km ✕; photograph page 4). Some 7km further on is the tourist pavilion at the **Baths of Aphrodite★** (✕ 📷 **P**20), where Walks 19, 20 and both versions of Alternative walk 21 converge.

Returning on the same road, those with 4WD vehicles may choose one of the options described on the next page, via Neokhorio, but if you are in a normal hire car you should come back through Lachi (64km) and Prodhromi to **Polis** (68km ▲ ✕ 🖃 🇮🇹), an appealing town of ancient origin, and once centre of a thriving copper mining industry. From here follow the signposted main road (B7) back towards Pafos, with optional short stops and detours. At **Skoulli** (78km), the Herpetological Society of Cyprus operates the second reptile exhibition on this tour. You may not be fond of these creatures, but it's useful to know what they look like!

A right turn at about 86km offers a detour to Miliou (▲ **P**23), a tiny Laona village noted for traditional weaving, and the start- and end-point for Walk 23. A few kilometres further on, a similar right turn leads to the totally abandoned village of Kato Theletra, where the threat of landslips led to mass evacuation a few decades

4WD OPTIONS

After visiting the Baths of Aphrodite, head back towards Lachi, but make a right turn and drive 3km to the village of **Neokhorio** (see reverse of touring map; normal hire cars can follow this stretch as well, but will need to return the same way). Drive carefully through the narrow, winding streets, passing the church on your right, and emerge at the other side of the village. Once clear of houses you will come to a fork in the road…

Route A is signposted to **Smiyies** and is a rough but level road leading in about 3km past the church of Ayios Minas to the Smiyies picnic site (⊞*P*21), a well-equipped and popular location where nature trails start and finish (see Walk 21). A well-shod hire car could make it this far but definitely *no further!*

Drive past the picnic site (on your right) and head for the T-junction on the skyline. Turn left, then, after a short distance, turn right in the direction of Koudounas (signposted). Keep going for just under 3km to another junction, where you again turn right towards Koudounas. This rough track (and it *is* rough!) winds westward toward the coast road which you reach some 6km beyond the T-junction at Smiyies. The views are wonderful.

Turn left and drive about 7km to **Lara Beach** (*P*14; Walk 14; photographs above and pages 78, 79). The track is rutted, but gives access to a number of secluded beaches where you could skinny-dip with impunity, or picnic to your heart's content.

From Lara, continue on the unmade road past the signposted Viklari taverna on your left and the turn-off to the Avagas Gorge (Walk 16; cover photograph). After 6km come into **Ayios Yeoryios**, now on an asphalted road.

From Ayios Yeoryios, where there is a small harbour, rock tombs and a church of 6th century origin, you have a simple drive of about 20km to **Pafos**, via Coral Bay and Kissonerga.

Route B follows Route A to the fork beyond **Neokhorio**. Here turn left past a goat enclosure and drive for 5km to the once-Turkish village of **Androlikou** (photograph page 81), which was abandoned during the Turkish occupation of the island in 1974. The village is now home to a single Cypriot family, a few sheep, a few pigs, a few noisy dogs … and around 1000 goats. After you've inspected the old houses, taken some photos, and assured the dogs that you're not Turkish, turn right to head for **Fasli** (now on asphalt). At a ridge 1km beyond Fasli, where a left turn would take you to Drousseia (see map pages 78-79), turn right along an appallingly rutted track for 1km, then turn left to gain wonderful views over the coastline. This track takes you to the coast road, just above **Lara Beach**. From here the return to **Pafos** is as described in Route A.

24

Above: spring on the Agias-mata nature trail at Kathikas (Walk and Picnic 12); right, from top to bottom: disused spring at Kato Arodhes; farmer at Akoursos; poppies and daisies; giant fennel (Ferula communis)

ago. It's an atmospheric place to explore (photographs page 99), but keep to the streets — the crumbling buildings could be unsafe. Old Theletra is the mid-point of Walk 23 — a superb hike.

Pass through **Stroumbi** (98km ✕) to reach **Mesoyi** (108km), from where a right turn would take you to the monastery of Ayios Neophytos (✝☎; Walk 11) — an optional detour of 8km return. From Mesoyi, it's a short drive back to the centre of **Pafos** (115km), after a day spent exploring a varied and unhurried region of the island.

2 OLD VILLAGES, ROCKS AND BONES!

Pafos • Yeroskipos • Kouklia • Pano Arkhimandrita • Dhora • Arsos • Omodhos • Episkopi • Kourion • Petra tou Romiou • Pafos

130km/81mi; about 3h30min driving; Exit A from Pafos

On route: Picnic (see pages 14-18) (18a, 18b); Walks 17, (18)

A full day's tour, packed with variety and interesting scenery — mostly on good asphalted roads (but sometimes on terrible ones!)

Head out of Pafos on the Lemesos road (Exit A; Leophoros Yeoryiou Griva Dhiyeni). The first village, effectively a suburb of Pafos, is **Yeroskipos** (3km **✝▲✕⛽M**), renowned for *loukoumi,* the delicacy shown opposite. Call it Turkish delight if you wish, but not within Greek earshot. One of only two surviving five-domed Byzantine churches on Cyprus stands here, Ayia Paraskevi. (The other, at Peristerona, is visited on Car tour 5; see drawing on page 34). Also of interest is the Folk Art Museum: housed in an 18th-century building, it holds an impressive collection of implements both domestic and agricultural, plus rural apparel.

Pass the airport turn-off at **Timi** and, beyond **Mandria** (⛽), turn left to **Kouklia★** (16km **∏✕M**), site of the Temple of Aphrodite and Ancient ('Palea') Pafos. It is likely that old Pafos was destroyed by earthquakes in the 12th century BC, and there is little for the casual visitor to see, but the temple and nearby medieval manor are impressive.

Drive slowly through Kouklia. Then a tortuous road takes you to **Pano Arkhimandrita** (30km). Walk 17 (an all-time favourite with 'Landscapers') starts here, and it is worthwhile to pause for a short time to visit the shrine of Ayii Pateres (see drawing on page 83) and view the scenery which is spectacular on all sides and brilliantly green in springtime (photograph pages 84-85).

The road continues on a rougher surface through tiny **Mousere** and skirts round **Dhora** (37km), to a junction (44km). Turn left and follow the sign to **Arsos** (48km), noted for its dark red wine. Enter the village if you wish, or simply follow the 'bypass', which brings you to a

Unusual sights always catch my eye. This 3m-high upright stone near Pakhna is pierced with a hole. A mystery. But one old Cyprus legend suggested that if a man could not crawl through such a gap, he had cuckold's horns!

Market stalls: loukoumi *(top);*
fruits and nuts

clear sign indicating a right
turn onto a rough road to
Omodhos (60km ♦✕M).
This larger village, too, is
famed for the quality of its
wine, and is well worth exploring. The pedestrianised
central area is a touch com-
mercial, but you have to buy
your wine, *soujoukko, loukoumi,* lace, postcards, olive
oil and terracotta pots somewhere, so why not here? Be
sure to wander the narrow streets, too, and observe how
exquisitely restored many of the houses are. The central
Monastery of Stavros is modern but worth inspecting.

On the far side of Omodhos, turn left on a fast road
signposted to Lemesos, passing turn-offs to Pakhna,
Ayios Amvrosios, Pano Kividhes and Kandou, before
hitting the coast road beyond the A6 motorway and
turning right to drive through **Episkopi** (83km ✕🚍M).
This is the centre of the British military presence on
Cyprus, one of two Sovereign Base Areas — the other
being at Dhekelia, east of Larnaka (Car tour 7).

Just beyond Episkopi is the ancient site of **Kourion★**
(**⒤**✕🖼), one of the most important excavations on the
island (open daily). Visit the tourist pavilion and acquire
all the information you need to make the most of your
visit to Kourion and the nearby **Temple of Apollo★** (**⒤**).
Then continue east above Pissouri, from where you
could make a detour to Alekhtora (*P*18a, 18b), either to
picnic or to enjoy a short walk overlooking the Khapotami Gorge (Walk 18).

Our last visit for today is to the famed **Rocks of
Aphrodite★** (103km ✕). There is a tourist pavilion for
your refreshment and enlightenment. It is said that the
Goddess of Love was born from the sea foaming against
the offshore rocks here (of which **Petra tou Romiou** is
one; 'petra' means stone). From the rocks, Aphrodite was
carried by a shell to the shore — a story most vividly
illustrated in Botticelli's painting, *The Birth of Venus.*

Not far beyond Aphrodite's rocks is the Kouklia turn-
off where we started up into the hills earlier in the day.
From here it's a straight run back to **Pafos** (130km).

3 LAND OF THE MOUFFLON

**Pafos • Polemi • Kannaviou • Stavros tis Psokas •
Dhodheka Anemi • Cedar Valley • Kykko Monastery •
Panayia • Chrysorroyiatissa Monastery • Statos • Pafos**

approximately 151km/94mi; about 4h driving; Exit B from Pafos

On route: ⌕ at Stavros Forestry Station, Cedar Valley; Picnic (see pages
14-18) 10; Walks 9, 10

*A full day's tour, partly on narrow, rough and winding mountain tracks,
only suitable for 4WD vehicles. The route is packed with variety and
beautiful landscapes, so allow plenty of time. Those in standard hire
cars can still enjoy much of the tour, by omitting Cedar Valley and
taking the alternative return route described on page 30.*

Take Exit B from Pafos (Leophoros Evagora Pallika-
ridis). Some 13km out of town, make a right turn (signposted) to **Polemi** (16km 🕮), a large grape-packing community, and from here continue to **Kannaviou** (24km ✗).

Some 1.2km beyond Kannaviou, turn left on a dirt
road towards 'Anadiou' and 'Sarama'. At the fork 1km
uphill, go right for 'Stavros', now on an almost-level and
well-graded, but narrow and winding mountain track. At
32km the interesting little church of Stavros tou Kratimaton (♟) is signposted 300m off to the right — a pleasant
picnic spot with benches. At 42km a track comes in from
the right — from the Ayia picnic site.

Stavros tis Psokas (45km ♠⌕) is named after a
monastery originally sited here, called Stavros tis Psoras
('Cross of the Measles'; the spring at Stavros reputedly
held holy water which cured that illness). The forests
around Stavros are home to the timid moufflon, but you
are more likely to see examples in captivity at the forest
station.

From Stavros continue uphill, observing on the right
the start of the Horteri nature trail (Walk 9), and come to
a road junction with comprehensive signposting. On the
left is another short nature trail ('Selladi tou Stavrou', also
described in Walk 9). Turn right here towards Kykko and
come after about 8km to a junction at **Dhodheka Anemi**
(55km). Park here for a moment and consider walking
the 4km to **Mount Tripylos** and back, to break up your
day. The views from this peak (1362m/4470ft; *P*10) are
magnificent. Walk 10 offers a long, but fairly easy circuit
in this area.

The road straight ahead leads to Kykko Monastery
after 17km; take this road if you are in a standard hire
car. But it is more scenic to take the signposted forest road
to the right — to **Cedar Valley**★ (65km ⌕), a lovely
remote region of tall, majestic cedars. This links up again

Top and left: Kykko Monastery is almost sumptuous in its decor, compared with more humble retreats. Above: the little church of Stavros tou Kratimaton on the track to Stavros is a pleasant place to stretch your legs

with the asphalt road from Dhodheka Anemi and then comes to a north/south road, where we turn right to **Kykko Monastery★** (84km ✝▲), famed throughout the Greek Orthodox world and one of the biggest land-owners on Cyprus. Kykko has an interesting history both ancient and recent; it contains, among other treasures, an icon attributed to St Luke.

Returning from Kykko, turn sharp right just past the tacky tourist kiosks, alongside the monastery wall. The road winds steeply uphill, past the ornate bell-tower shown overleaf, to **Throni★** (85.5km 📷), the mountain-top tomb of Archbishop Makarios, from where the views are superb.

From Throni the main tour follows a *very* rough track. Head back through the one-way system at Kykko and

Bell-tower on the road to Throni

turn right when you reach the main road.* At the next junction (having passed the kiosks again), turn left. Then, at the first left-hand hairpin bend, go straight across towards 'Myli-kouri'. Immediately, turn right on an asphalt road signposted to the Vryssi Restaurant. After the restaurant the way becomes very rough and narrow. Follow this track for 16km — to the first fork, where you should turn right. Turn left after 5km at the next fork, and left again — to come to **Pano Panayia** (119km), the birthplace of Makarios, where you meet surfaced road.

Beyond Panayia, you have three options for your return to Pafos. You can continue on the good road through Asproyia to Kannaviou, from there retracing the outward journey. But you may wish to see **Chrysorro-yiatissa Monastery★** (⛪🛏🍽), only 1.5km from Panayia. From the monastery head south to **Statos**, then *either* proceed via Pendalia and the E606 to the coast road and turn right; *or* head for the Pafos-Polis road via Khoulou, Letimbou and Tsadha. Each of the three options brings you back to **Pafos** after about 151km, rounding off a perhaps tiring but spectacular day in high and holy places.

---

*Alternative return on asphalt roads:** If you are in a standard hire car, from Throni retrace your route back to **Stavros**. Then take the Lyso road (next to the café and forestry station). Newly asphalted, this good road winds through thickly forested slopes, with fine views to the mountains and a heady aroma of conifers. Ignore left turns to Sarama and Melandra. Beyond a monument to the EOKA fighters (121km), you come into **Lyso** (124km 🍽), a lovely hilltop village with a cultural centre and several tavernas.

Take the road to Polis on leaving the village, passing **Meladeia** (🛏) before reaching **Peristerona** (126km **M** — not to be confused with the Peristerona near Lefkosia, which is visited on Car tour 5). Together with Lyso, this was a base for the EOKA. It is worth a stop to visit the Byzantine Museum and to view the **Atichoulli Gorge** on the right at the end of the village. Many caves where the fighters lived are visible in the rock face of the gorge, but these cliffs are now the nesting sites of raptors and smaller birds. On leaving Peristerona, look for a sharp left turn, signed 'Pafos' (127km), and follow this tarred road (🛏) above the **Evretou Dam** to the main Polis/Pafos road (B7; 130km). Turn left for the trip back to Pafos (157km).

4 FROM PAFOS TO PLATRES

Pafos • Asprokremnos Dam • Nikouklia • Phasoula • Ayios Yeoryios • Kithasi • Kedhares • Ayios Nikolaos • Pera Pedi • Saittas • Platres

approximately 67km/41mi; about 1h30min driving; Exit A from Pafos

On route: 🅟 around Troodos (see map pages 54-55); Picnics (see pages 14-18) 1-5, 8; Walks 1-6; 8

An easy but pretty drive from Pafos through a picturesque river valley into the Troodos foothills, where you can link up with Car tour 5 if you wish to continue to Lefkosia, and a choice of return routes to Pafos.

It's a lot easier that it once was to reach the Troodos Mountains from Pafos. There is still no *fast* way of doing it, but who wants one?

This is arguably the most direct route, and it is certainly an attractive morning's drive. Leave Pafos at Exit A on the Lemesos road, and take the first major left turn after the airport turn-off. It is signposted to the **Asprokremnos Dam**, which is reached at about 14km. This is one of the larger (and newer) reservoirs on the island, and you should cross the dam wall very slowly, because the speed-reducing ramps are quite severe. Turn left on the far side and come to **Nikouklia**.

You are in the beautiful Dhiarizos Valley, and you may observe the abandoned village of Souskiou across the river (which may be bone dry late in the year). Beyond **Phasoula** (25km), with its disused mosque, proceed very easily through **Ayios Yeoryios**, **Kithasi** and **Kedhares** to **Ayios Nikolaos** (44km) which offers a choice of tavernas and some lovely views westward over the upper valley.

After leaving Ayios Nikolaos, start to get impressive

In the beautiful Dhiarizos Valley

The harbour at Pafos, where you're likely to see sponge divers and fishermen. Speciments of all sizes are available here; the larger sponges are not cheap, but they are a lot less expensive than they would be back home.

views of the Troodos Mountains. Continue to **Mandria**, then turn right to **Pera Pedi** (56km; *P*8 and Walk 8) and **Saittas** (✕*P*4). Turn left to **Platres★** (67km ▲▲ ✕ ➌ ▣ ⊕). This mountain resort has all the facilities you could want, and nearby are many walk options (*P*1-5; Walks 1-6; see area map pages on 54-55 and photographs on pages 51-61).

You can now follow Car tour 5 for a run of about 80km via Troodos to Lefkosia on good roads. But there are several appealing options for a return drive to Pafos.

Option 1: Follow the early section of Car tour 5 in reverse from Platres to Lemesos (about 40km), then it's another 72km along the coast road back to Pafos.

Option 2: Retrace your route as far as Mandria, then follow signs to Omodhos, from where you can drive part of Car tour 2 in reverse — via Mallia, Dhora, and Pano Arkhimandrita. When you reach the coast road at Kouklia, return to Pafos (about 130km in total).

Option 3: For a really full day's sightseeing, set off early from Pafos to Platres and Troodos, then drive via Prodhromos and Pedhoulas to Kykko Monastery and Stavros. To finish, follow the asphalt road return for Car tour 3 back to Pafos (see notes at the foot of page 30), making a splendid 'Grand Tour' of around 150km covering the west of the island.

5 A CAPITAL CIRCUIT

Lemesos • Trimiklini • Platres • Troodos • Kakopetria • Galata • Peristerona • Lefkosia • (Stavrovouni Monastery) • Lemesos

approximately 200km/125 mi; about 4-5h driving; Exit A from Lemesos

On route: ⊼ at Platania and Passia's Meadow (both north of Troodos towards Kakopetria on the west side of the road), also Kornos Forestry Station a few miles from Stavrovouni; Picnics (see pages 14-18) 1-5, (7, 8, 25a, 25b, 27); Walks 1-6, (7, 8, 24, 25, 27). (Walk 26 is also best reached from Lemesos.)

A long circuit with many optional detours. Quite easy to accomplish in one day if you like driving, but impossible if you want to do a lot of exploring. It makes an excellent two-day outing with an overnight stay in Lefkosia. All roads are asphalted.

Driving in Lemesos is not for the faint-hearted! The town's traffic management leaves much to be desired, and one should especially be wary of kamikaze moped riders. But here is an escape from such urban perils. Leave the bustling environs of Lemesos at the Polemidhia roundabout (Exit A; junction with Makarios Avenue) and follow the Platres and Troodos sign. The road, still narrow in places, has been much improved to allow comparatively swift transit from the coast to the mountains in barely an hour. Pass Polemidhia Dam on your left after a few kilometres, then Kouris Dam, before reaching **Trimiklini** (30km ✕).

After Trimiklini, continue through **Saittas** (✕; easy access to Walk 8 and *P*4, *P*8) and **Moniatis** before coming into **Platres**★ (37km ▲▲✕➔⊕). This resort is fragmented around the pine-clad hillsides at an invigorating altitude of 1100m/3600ft. Park awhile, and at least explore the central area where you will find shops, banks and a tourist information office. You may also care to look at the Forest Park Hotel, where Daphne Du Maurier wrote the novel *Rebecca*.

You might turn to pages 54-55 before resuming your journey. It is obvious from this 1:50,000 scale map of the Troodos region that Platres is an excellent centre for walkers (especially those with a hire car), and there are many hotels in the area, of all categories. Walks 3 and 4 finish in the centre near the Tourist Information Office; Walk 6 is a short drive away.

From Platres the tour continues up to the trout farm (**Psilon Dhendron**; *P*3; *P*5; Walks 3, 5) and **Troodos** (45km ▲▲✕➔). The air is pine-fresh and you are just 3-4km from the summit of Mount Olympus★ (⊓➔*P*1) to the northwest, one of the

The priest at Nikitari holds the keys to this church (above) at Asinou, the finest Byzantine church on Cyprus. Murals cover the interior.

Cyprus has hundreds of churches, ranging from tiny bare chapels in remote villages to ornately-decorated edifices containing priceless artefacts. You are likely to come upon long-ruined Byzantine churches with ages-old wall and ceiling paintings still visible. Many an old building is used by shepherds for shelter… for themselves or for their sheep and goats!

It is an unusual village that does not have a church of some kind. If the church is closed, and you would like to see inside it, ask at the local café, where they will

readily raise the priest or caretaker, who will open the church for you. If you are exploring a place of worship, remember to dress in suitable clothing. It is also useful to carry a torch for the inspection of dark interiors.

Not every church is distinctive, but that of St Barnabas (Ayii Varnava) at Peristerona, shown below, certainly is. Its five-domed structure dates back to the 10th century, and there is only one other five-domed church on Cyprus — at Yeroskipos (Car tour 2).

There are mosques in Greek Cyprus, too, but almost all have remained closed since 1974 (a notable exception being Hala Sultan Tekke, of course: see Car tour 6).

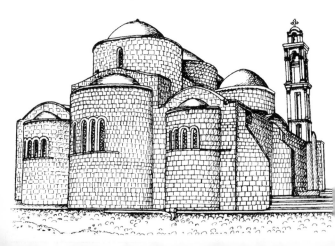

optional detours on this tour. This is the highest point on Cyprus, at 1952m/6400ft. The island's short skiing season (January to March) is centred on its slopes; there is also a radar installation, a TV mast and the remains of a Venetian tower. Walk 1 is a lovely way of experiencing Mount Olympus.

From Troodos, Walk 2 is an easy leg-stretcher and offers splendid views to the northeast (**P**2) and the route we are about to cover. The road sweeps past the Pano Amiandos mine on the right and the turn-off to Kype-rounda (**P**7; Walk 7); note that there is a petrol station (🛢) 200m down the Saittas road to the right at this point. You will see two official picnic sites to the left (🛱) before coming into **Kakopetria** (60km 🛉🛌✕🛢 and 🛉 Ayios Nikolaos 3km southwest) and **Galata** (64km 🛉🛌✕) — foothill villages which both reward exploration if you have the time, especially if you enjoy old churches.

This route (B9) goes straight to Peristerona, but consider first a 28km return detour to Asinou church★ (see panel opposite) from the Koutraphas crossroads, via Nikitari. Beyond **Peristerona** (85km 🛉), head straight for **Lefkosia**★ (117km 🛉🛉🛌✕🛢⊕🎏M), the attractions, sights and peculiarities of which are fully detailed in tourist office material. If you are staying overnight, you might consider a brief crossing (on foot) into the Turkish-occupied area at the Ledra checkpoint, and you should certainly see the colourful Laiti Yitonia area near the city centre, the Venetian walls, the Cyprus Museum, and the ancient Cathedral of St John.

Leaving Lefkosia on Archbishop Makarios Avenue (Exit A on the town plan on pages 8-9), reach the A1 for a swift return to Lemesos in an hour or so. But a detour of about 18km return to Stavrovouni Monastery★ (**P**27 and Walk 27; Car tour 6; photographs pages 37, 111) is highly recommended. Other possible excursions off this route include the lace-making centre of Lefkara, but this could prove costly, as the good people of Lefkara will do their utmost to persuade you to spend!

You may care to dally at Governor's Beach (Walk 24), where there are facilities of a ramshackle nature, or call at the Monastery of Ayios Yeoryios Alamanou. Walk 24 starts at this distinctive blue and white retreat, shown on page 101. Beyond here you pass the turning to Kellaki (photograph page 103), from where Walk 25 descends to the Yermasoyia Dam (photograph pages 106-107; **P**25a) outside **Lemesos** (about 200km, *without detours*).

6 THE HEIGHT OF ORTHODOXY

Larnaka • Hala Sultan Tekke • Kiti • Dhromolaxia • Kalokhorio • Pyrga • Stavrovouni Monastery • Kophinou • Larnaka

approximately 100km/62mi; about 3h driving; Exit B from Larnaka

On route: ⊼ at the Kornos Forestry Station a few miles from Stavrovouni; Picnic (see pages 14-18) 27, 28; Walks 27, 28

A full day out from Larnaka, taking in a Moslem holy place, one of the finest churches on Cyprus and the pinnacle of Stavrovouni. All roads are asphalted. **Note: Women are not allowed to enter Stavrovouni, neither is photography permitted.**

Take the road south to the airport (Exit B) for the start of this compact tour, and notice the shimmering whiteness of the Salt Lake, which is exploited commercially in the summer months. In winter it rains and the lake fills up, becoming a refuge for thousands of flamingoes and other migratory birds.

Just past the airport, turn right to palm-shrouded **Hala Sultan Tekke★** (5km ♨️⛩️✕), the third most important place of Moslem pilgrimage, after Mecca and Medina. It is a shrine revered as the burial place of the prophet Mohammed's aunt. Take off your shoes and go inside…

'Twas in the mid-7th century during an Arab raid on the island that Umm Haram, maternal aunt of the prophet, was travelling with her husband when she fell from her mule and broke her neck. She was buried at once 'in that fragrant spot'. The location, shown below, is indeed beautiful, with the mosque and its minaret surrounded by gardens and trees. It is as much frequented by tourists as pilgrims these days, and there is a restaurant

Hala Sultan Tekke and the Salt Lake

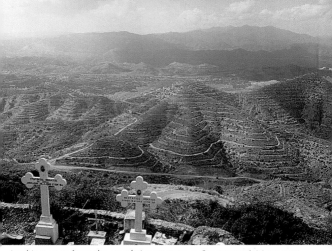

Looking west from the monks' cemetery at Stavrovouni Monastery, where photography, regrettably, is no longer permitted.

nearby. Excavations to the west of the mosque have revealed the site of a Bronze Age town and many historically valuable artefacts.

After visiting the Tekke ... put your shoes on again and return to the main road, turning right to reach **Kiti** village (11km ♦✕), which is notable only for the church shown on page 114 — the magnificent Panayia Angeloktistos★ ('built by angels'). It houses the finest Byzantine mosaics on Cyprus. Walk 28, which takes in a Venetian watchtower and another lovely church (photographs page 113) starts and ends nearby. If you've packed bathing things, you might like to try a short version of this hike (*P*28).

Come back on the same road as far as **Meneou**, then turn left to pass through **Dhromolaxia**, shortly reaching a crossroads, at which keep ahead to **Kalokhorio** (26km ♦). Head for **Ayia Anna**, then **Pyrga** (35km ♦✕).

Some 1.5km beyond Pyrga you will meet the old Lefkosia/Lemesos road (⌂ near the Kornos Forestry Station). Turn left and after another 1.5km find the signposted turn-off left to Stavrovouni. The monastery is reached after an unprepossessing drive of 10km — past a quarry and an army camp (remember not to take photographs in this area). **Stavrovouni Monastery**★ (48km ♦⌨*P*27) is the goal of Walk 27. The approach is by way of a series of hairpin bends, but the road (once a rough track) is now asphalted. The views (see photographs above and on page 111) are astounding.

After your visit, follow the *old* Lemesos road south as far as **Kophinou** (70km ✕), and then turn left for a straight run back to **Larnaka** (about 100km).

37

7 THE FAR EAST

Larnaka • Dhekelia crossroads • Phrenaros • Dherinia • Paralimni • Protaras • Cape Greco • Ayia Napa • Xylophagou • Larnaka

100km/62mi; about 3h driving; Exit A from Larnaka

On route: 🅿 at Xylotimbou; Picnics (see pages 14-18) 29, 30; Walks 29, 30

A full day, offering a variety of popular beaches, quiet seaside picnic spots, country roads … and a view across the 'green line' to forbidden Famagusta. All roads are asphalted; a few are narrow.

Hit the Dhekelia road north out of Larnaka (Makarios III; Exit A), first passing a light industrial area, with petroleum storage tanks much in evidence. But having left these behind, you are heading for the southeastern extremity of Cyprus, which boasts the best beaches and accompanying crowds, but has a quiet charm, too. A wide variety of produce is grown in the rich red soil. Water is a precious commodity at the agricultural end of the island, and windmills abound, drawing water out of the ground to irrigate crops of potatoes and other vegetables.

As the industrial area ends, the beaches start, and to your right you will see a shoreline which is recreational for several kilometres, offering watersports, hotels, apartments and restaurants.

The hot Cyprus sun can do strange things to one's body. Here at Nissi Beach, as afternoon shadows lengthen, these sunseekers are oblivious to the way they look after hours of trying to achieve a golden-brown, all-over tan. Very easy to do at Nissi, but don't stay too long. Meanwhile, the fellow at the top obviously has a touch of sunstroke. He thinks he has scored with a beach beauty. But don't squeeze too hard, friend, or the lady will go to pieces…

The **Dhekelia crossroads** (14km) lead eastward to the British Sovereign Base Area, but you should head north here, following the signposting for Famagusta. The road bends around Xylotimbou (⊞) and then Athna (which is inaccessible, being over the 'green line' in the Turkish zone). Our route passes through a corridor of the Sovereign Base Area, leading almost to Ayios Nikolaos.

Turn right short of 'Aye Nick' (as the locals call it) and head for **Phrenaros** (38km) and from there to **Dherinia** (42km ✕). From the northern side of this village, one can get a clear view of Turkish-occupied Famagusta only a few kilometres distant. In the opposite direction (our continuing route) lies the larger village of **Paralimni** (45km ▲✕▣). Follow the signs for Protaras and Cape Greco for a few kilometres, almost on the coast, passing through an area noted for its forest of windmills — a vital part of the irrigation system in this agricultural region.

At **Protaras★** (57km ✝▲✕) there is an excellent beach and ancillary development which mushroomed in the early 1980s. Be sure not to miss the church of Profitis Ilias while you're here. The whole area between Protaras (or 'Fig Tree Bay', as it is also called) and Ayia Napa is splendid for picnicking and walking. Those who want a real constitutional can combine Walks 29 and 30. For

View to Cape Greco from Ayia Napa (Picnic 29)

suggestions, a large-scale map, and more photographs of this area, see pages 115 to 120.

The road continues south, turns sharp right above Cape Greco and the Radio Monte Carlo transmitter masts, and continues to **Ayia Napa**★ (66km ✝🏔✕🅿⊕ *P*29, *P*30), another much-developed tourist area, thanks to its fine beaches. At the centre of Ayia Napa is an again-thriving monastery, used now as an ecumenical centre. Note the 600-year-old sycamore at its entrance.

The return to Larnaka passes the turn-off to Nissi Beach, heading then via **Xylophagou** (78km ✕), a market-gardening centre, and **Dhekelia** (86km) back to **Larnaka** (100km).

Walking

In this Fourth edition of the first-ever walkers' guide to Cyprus, I describe routes covering more than 300 kilometres (200 miles) of the best rambling on the island.

The walks are designed to show you as painlessly as possible the wide variety of Cyprus landscape and to take you through a few communities not often troubled by the conventional tourist trade. In these villages, you will find the island at its most heartwarming. Here, a rambler with boots and rucksack might attract a few quizzical looks (Cypriots are strangers to walking for pleasure!), but the welcome will be genuine and hospitality generous to those who rest awhile.

I have indicated on the walking maps and in the notes where walks can be linked to create a more strenuous option, and any overlap or proximity of walks is easily seen on the fold-out touring map, where the walks are highlighted in white. But a word of caution: **never try to get from one walk to another on uncharted terrain**. Link walks only by following routes indicated in the walking notes or by following roads or tracks. Do not try to cross rough country: this could be dangerous, or you might not have right of way.

Beginners: Many of the walks are easily accomplished by novices, providing you are sensibly shod and equipped. Check the short walk options and picnic suggestions for even easier rambles.

Experienced walkers: All the walks in the book should be within your stride, even the occasional bit of scrambling.

All walkers: Please follow the routes as described in the notes, and if you are at any stage uncertain of the way forward, go back to the last 'sure' point and think again. Do **not** try to continue a walk where natural damage (such as a landslide) has made the way impassable or dangerous. Bulldozers have the same effect!

Waymarking and maps

The authorities on Cyprus acknowledge that walking is a popular pursuit and have gone to great lengths to **signpost** and **waymark** walking routes and nature trails. However, it is not always easy to locate the start of their trails, and waymarking is sadly lacking at many junctions along the way. Tracks abound in rural areas, but they often lead only to vineyards or goat enclosures and can be confusing.

For all the routes described in the book, the **maps** accompanying the text should suffice. They are based on notes made 'in the field' and were prepared with reference to a set of 1:25,000-scale maps published in 1960 and obtained from the Department of Lands and Surveys in Lefkosia. If you can obtain them, the British D Survey/Ministry of Defence Series K717 maps (scale 1:50,000) are more up to date (1970s), but are not on general sale. Unfortunately both of these sets of maps, although very useful for seeing the 'lie of the land', are now hopelessly out of date regarding roads, tracks and paths.

The nature trail guides published by the Cyprus Tourism Organisation contain very basic sketch maps of their trails, with brief general comments, but no walk *directions;* ask for these at the tourist offices in the main resorts — especially early in the year, when smaller tourist offices may not yet be open.

Where to stay

For purely a walking holiday on Cyprus, the obvious area to head for is the mountainous **Troodos region**. Its focal point is Mount Olympus, and within a 25km radius you have a wide choice of walking opportunities. I have described the more accessible routes.

Platres, a hill resort with shops, restaurants, banks, hotels and apartments, is the most popular centre, but there are others — Troodos, Prodhromos, Pedhoulas and Kakopetria among them.

The Cyprus Tourism Organisation publishes annually a list of places to stay in the Troodos region and every other resort on the island. It covers accommodation ranging from five-star luxury hotels to economical self-catering apartments.

There is **good coastal walking**, plus splendid beaches, around the Ayia Napa/Protaras area on the southeastern corner of the island. To the southwest there is pleasant strolling around Pafos. Interesting walking excurions can be made from Larnaka (notably to Stavrovouni, but also out to the southeast). If you're based at Lemesos, the Troodos region is reached in under an hour by road.

But increasingly, walking enthusiasts are enjoying the **Akamas Peninsula** in the northwest corner of the island, an hour or less from Pafos. You will need your own transport to do this area justice, and I would recommend hiring a 4WD vehicle. The hills, valleys, gorges and wild coastline around places like Polis, Lachi, Drousseia, Kathikas and Lara are completely unspoiled.

Basic accommodation may be available at some (but not all) of the island's **monasteries**, but bedding is *not* provided. No charge is made, but a donation on departure is appreciated. This privilege is really intended for Greek Orthodox pilgrims, and as a tourist, if you really want somewhere cheap to stay, it is more appropriate to seek out a room in a village. This is a great help to the fragile rural economy, and you will get a good deal and a cheap, authentic Cypriot meal.

Accommodation for a maximum of three nights is available at the **Stavros Forestry Station** (see page 67); book in advance (tel 26-332144 or 26-722338).

A highly satisfying way of exploring Cyprus on foot for

Goats on the Akamas uplands, in mist

the first time would be to **combine a week in the Troodos with a week on the coast**. That way, you would have time for some of that sun, sand and brandy sour!

Weather

The Cyprus climate is splendidly Mediterranean, with constant sunshine during much of the year, and with rainfall being confined to a fairly short and predictable winter, when temperatures remain at a pleasurable level.

The walker probably experiences Cyprus at its climatic best between March and early summer, when the countryside is a blaze of floral colour and the sun hot, but not unbearably so. September and October are good walking months too.

The high Troodos region is cold in winter (and can be so beyond Easter), with snow usually allowing skiing for about eight weeks on the slopes of Mount Olympus. Summer temperatures here can be high, but they are usually a few refreshing degrees cooler than on the coast and consistently cooler than in Lefkosia, where the mercury can go above 38°C (100°F) for days on end!

Important: Anyone planning a walking trip early in the year should note that rainfall can turn dry tracts into streams and rivers. Moreover, there might still be snow in the mountains, making it impossible to follow some walks and tours.

AVERAGE TEMPERATURES

Month	Average air temperature				Average sea temperature		%age of days with sun
	Min		Max				
	°C	°F	°C	°F	°C	°F	
Jan	8.9	47.9	18.3	65	16.5	61.4	57
Feb	9.4	49	19.4	66.9	16.9	62.4	63
Mar	10	50	20.6	69.1	17.3	63.2	67
Apr	12.2	53.9	22.8	73.1	18.6	65.5	71
May	15.6	60.1	27.2	81	21.1	69.9	79
Jun	18.3	65	30	85.9	24	75.3	87
Jul	22.8	73.1	35.6	96	26	79.4	90
Aug	22.8	73.1	35.6	96	27.8	81.9	88
Sep	18.3	65	32.2	90	27.6	80	88
Oct	17.2	63	27.8	82	25.1	77	80
Nov	12.2	53.9	23.9	75	21.9	71.4	71
Dec	8.3	46.9	17.2	66	18.9	66.4	59

What to take

If you are already on Cyprus when you find this book and do not have items like a rucksack or walking boots, you can still enjoy a number of the easier walks, or you can buy some equipment in one of the sports shops. Please do not attempt the longer or more difficult walks without the proper equipment. For each walk described, the absolute minimum equipment is given. Do adjust the equipment according to the season; for instance, take a long-sleeved shirt and long trousers, as well as a sunhat, in summer months, and a fleece and raingear on cooler days.

Where walking boots are prescribed, there is, unfortunately, no substitute. You will need to rely on their grip and ankle protection and, occasionally, their waterproof qualities. If you do wear shoes, make sure they have rubber soles, preferably of the Vibram or Skywalk variety. The often stony and dusty tracks of Cyprus can be unforgiving toward the improperly shod walker.

Bear in mind, if you would, that I have not done *all* the walks in this book under *all* weather conditions. I may not realise just how hot or how wet a walk can be, depending on the season.

Nevertheless, if you intend going to Cyprus properly kitted out, you may find the following checklist useful. I rely on your good judgment to modify your equipment according to circumstances and the season. It is always wise to seek out local advice about conditions before undertaking any walk, especially in the hills.

walking boots (which must be broken-in and comfortable)
waterproof gear (outside summer months)
torch (if only for inspecting the darkened interiors of ruined churches!)
long-sleeved shirt (for sun protection)
long trousers, tight at the ankles
trekking pole(s)
small/medium-sized rucksack
up-to-date transport timetables
safety pins, string, clips

lightweight jacket
knives and openers
first aid kit
plastic groundsheet
plastic cups, plates, bottles
extra pairs of socks
anorak (zip opening)
warm fleece
plastic rainhat
sunhat, suncream
extra bootlaces
whistle, compass
telephone numbers of taxi operators and mobile phone

Walkers' checklist

The following cannot be stressed too often:

- **NEVER walk alone** — four is the best walking group.
- **If a walk becomes unsafe**, do not try to press ahead.
- **Do not overestimate your energy.** Your speed will be determined by the slowest walker in your group.
- **Transport connections** at the end of a walk are very important.

- **Proper shoes** or boots are vital.
- **Always take a sunhat** with you, and in summer a cover-up for your arms and legs as well.
- **Warm clothing** is needed in the mountains, especially in case you are delayed.
- **Mists** can fall suddenly in the mountains.
- **Always carry water and rations** on long walks.
- In spring, normally-dry **riverbeds may be flooded**.
- **Compass, whistle, torch** weigh little, but could save your life.
- **A stout stick** (or trekking pole) is a help on rough terrain and to discourage the rare unfriendly dog.
- **Do not panic** in an emergency.
- **Re-read the important note** on page 2 and the guidelines on grade and equipment for each walk you do.

Nuisances

Thankfully there are few nuisances to worry about when walking on Cyprus, but some walkers might favour carrying a stick or trekking pole: this could be of help on gradients and in the vicinity of goat enclosures, which are often guarded by noisy **dogs**. The best solution is to keep your stick out of sight, only using it defensively if absolutely necessary.

It should be noted that poisonous **snakes** are indigenous to the island, along with non-venomous varieties (see page 6 under 'Books': *Nature of Cyprus*). The chances of an encounter are slim, as snakes are shy creatures. As a precaution, however, it is wise to check under rocks or logs (perhaps with your stick) before settling down for a picnic, especially if you are somewhere very hot, close to water. Examples of all Cyprus reptiles, including snakes, are on view at the Herpetological Society's snake centre at Skoulli (near Polis on the road to Pafos) and at a similar centre between Coral Bay and Ayios Yeoryios (behind the petrol station).

Lizards of all shapes and sizes abound, but these are good fun!

Photography

Photography is forbidden in some sensitive areas (eg near military bases or the 'green line'), but warning signs make any restrictions clear. Some museums and churches do not allow photography … it is good manners to ask, in any case.

Greek for walkers

In the major tourist areas you hardly need to know any Greek at all, but once you are out in the countryside, a few words of the language will be helpful, and people will be grateful for your attempts to communicate.

Here's one way to ask directions in Greek and understand the answers you get! First memorise the few 'key' questions given below. Then, always follow up your key question with a second question demanding a yes ('ne') or no ('ochi') answer. Greeks invariably raise their heads to say 'no', which looks to us like the beginning of a 'yes'!

Following are the two most likely situations in which you may have to use some Greek. The dots (…) show where you will fill in the name of your destination. I'd recommend that you purchase an inexpensive phrase book: many give easily understood pronunciation hints, as well as a selection of phrases.

■ ASKING THE WAY
Key questions

English	Approximate Greek pronunciation
Good day, greetings	**Hair**-i-tay
Hello, hi (informal)	**Yas**-sas (plural); **Yia**-soo (singular)
Please — where is	**Sas** pa-ra-ka-**loh** — **pou ee**-nay
the road that goes to …?	o **thro**-mo stoh …?
the footpath that goes to …?	ee mono-**pati** stoh …?
the bus stop?	ee **sta**-ssis?
Many thanks.	Eff-hah-ree-**stoh** po-**li**.

Secondary question leading to a yes/no answer

Is it	**Ee**-nay
here?/there?/straight ahead?/	e-**tho**?/eh-**kee**?/kat-eff-**thia**?/
behind?/to the right?/	**pee**-so?/thex-**ya**?/
to the left?/above?/below?	aris-teh-**rah**?/eh-**pano**?/**kah**-to?

■ ASKING A TAXI DRIVER TO TAKE YOU/COLLECT YOU

Please —	**Sas** pa-ra-ka-**loh** —
would you take us to …?	Tha **pah**-reh mas stoh … ?
Come and pick us up	**El**-la na mas -reh-teh
from … (place) at … (time)*	apo … stees …*

*Point on your watch to the time you wish to be collected

Organisation of the walks

Each ramble in this book was chosen for its accessibility from one or more of the main tourist centres on Cyprus. Walks 1-8 are ideal for anyone staying in the **Troodos/Platres** area. Walks 9-10 are accessible too, but are set in mountainous country, remote from any major centres, and a considerable journey is necessary to reach them, wherever you are based. From **Pafos**, Walks 11-13 are nearest, but if you have a car consider too

Walks 9 and 10, 17 and 18, and *all* walks west of the Polis road (B7). From **Polis and Lachi**, Walks 15 and 19-23 are close at hand, but Walks 9 and 10 and all routes north of Paphos are easily reached by car. **Lemesos** is the recommended base for Walks 24-26, but Walks 1-8 and 17 and 18 are within reasonable driving distance. Walks 27 (Stavrovouni Monastery) and 28 are best approached from **Larnaka**, but Walk 27 is worth some kind of excursion from *wherever* you are staying! Walks 29 and 30 in the **Ayia Napa** region are also accessible from Larnaka.

I hope the book is set out so you can plan your walks easily. You might begin by considering the colour fold-out map inside the back cover. Here you can see at a glance the overall terrain, the road network, and the location of all the walks. Flipping through the book, you will also find at least one photograph for each walk. Having selected a potential excursion from the map and the photographs, look over the planning information at the beginning of the walk. Here you'll find distance/ hours, grade, equipment, and how to get there and return (by public and private transport). Wherever feasible, I have also suggested a short version of the walk, for those lacking in time and/or ability.

When you are on the walk, you will find that the text begins with an introduction to the overall landscape and then quickly turns to a detailed description of the route itself. The **large-scale maps** (all 1:50,000) have been annotated to show key landmarks. Times are given for reaching certain points on the walk. Giving times is always tricky, because they depend on so many factors, but the times I give are rather slower than my own walking time. Note that they **do not include any stops**! Allow ample time for photography and pottering about.

These symbols are used on the walking maps:

═══	motorway	●→	spring, tank, etc	■	castle, fort
▬▬▬	main road	✝✝	church.chapel	■	specified building
▬▬▬	secondary road	✝	shrine or cross	☗	transmitter mast
▒▒▒	unsurfaced road	⊡	cemetery	∩⊁	cave.windmill
▬▬▬	jeep track	⋒	picnic tables	⚒☀	quarry, mine.mill
┅┅┅	path, trail	⬛	best views	⬒	watchtower
—²→	main walk	🚌	bus stop	⊟	stadium
⋯²→	alternative walk	🚗	car parking	⚲	fire-watch tower
┅┅┅┅	other CTO trail	⊺	CTO signpost	⋔	ancient site
—400—	height (50 m intervals)	⊺	military warning sign	*P*	picnic suggestion
▥	map continuation	○	radar 'golf balls'		(see pages 14-18)

1 TROODOS • CHROMION • MOUNT OLYMPUS • TROODOS

See map pages 54-55; see also photographs on pages 2 and 56

Distance: 15km/9.3mi; 4h (add 1h return for the summit detour)

Grade: quite easy; gentle ups and downs between 1700m and 1750m

Equipment: walking boots or stout shoes, fleece, sunhat, water, picnic; waterproof in winter

How to get there and return: 🚗 to/from Troodos. A hire car gives greatest flexibility, but a shared private taxi from and back to Lemesos is a reasonable option. There is a 🚌 from Lemesos to Platres (Timetable B7), but no same-day return at time of writing; recheck schedules with the tourist office. If you do travel by bus, take a taxi from Platres to Troodos to start the walk, and arrange a return pickup at Troodos.

Shorter walk: Troodos to Chromion (9km/5.6mi; 2h30min; easy). Follow the main walk to Chromion and meet your taxi there.

Alternative walk: Artemis trail (7km/4.3mi; 2h; quite easy, with gentle ups and downs between 1800m and 1850m). 🚗 to the start of the nature trail, some 0.4km up the road to the Olympus summit.

There is a riding stable at Troodos, so the description of 'one horse town' is not entirely accurate. But it nearly fits. Despite recent 'improvements', Troodos is neither a town nor a village, but a collection of shops, small hotels, cafés and souvenir stalls. Even the open-air kebab houses and their squabbling owners have given way to a new rest area. I miss them! Troodos is a community that springs to life in summer and at weekends and is the centre of activity during Cyprus's short ski season. Four kilometres from Troodos by road is the highest point on the island — Mount Olympus (1952m/6400ft), the focal point of this, one of my favourite walks in the Troodos region. Though romantically named, the 'top of Cyprus' serves a prosaic function as the site of a TV transmitter and radar installation — the latter featuring enormous 'golf balls' which are a distinctive landmark. One does not have to go right to the summit on this walk, but it would be a pity not to do so, having come this far.

The walk starts at an INFORMATION BOARD for the **Atalante nature trail**, opposite the POST OFFICE/TELEPHONE EXCHANGE BUILDING at the northern end of the main (and only) street through **Troodos**. If you have the CTO's trail leaflet, prepare to be educated as well as invigorated…

At about **8min** the path curves round the back of the JUBILEE HOTEL, much favoured by skiers and walkers. The trail doubles back on itself at the head of a small 'gulch', which is a dry as a bone most of the year. Keep left at a fork (the right option leads to the Artemis trail … and is also our return route). As the trail contours at about 1750m, soon you can look south towards Platres and beyond. At about **25min** a wide panorama opens up, with even the Salt Lake at Lemesos visible on a clear day.

At **45min** you reach a THREE-WAY SIGNPOST and an open area with picnic potential and striking views (Picnic 1). Ignore the wide track up to the right and follow the trail past a wooden bench. Near trail point No 25, observe a stream of drinking water on the right (but it may be dry during summer). Follow the trail past a viewpoint at No 31, and come at No 37 to the tunnel entrance to the HADJIPAVLOU CHROMIUM MINE, which was worked from the 1950s until 1982. Keep out, if you have any sense! But you'll find shade here for a refreshment stop. Come soon to a signpost and follow the 'CHROMION' path to the left.

Beyond a stand of junipers (*Juniperus foetidissima*), screech to a halt near trail point No 48 (**1h50min**), to observe to your left Prodhromos village and the distinctive, abandoned Berengaria Hotel. On the horizon you'll see Throni, the peak above Kykko Monastery where Archbishop Makarios is buried. At **2h05min** the way becomes a little scree-like for a short distance. A few minutes later, notice a small abandoned QUARRY to the right; then, further on, look up the hillside for a clear view of the Mount Olympus TV mast.

Chromion, the end of the nature trail, comes up at around **2h30min**. Exit here the weary, the sun-struck and the tight of schedule. Onward to Olympus the rest of us! *Ignore* the road ahead; instead, bear right uphill on a faint LINK TRAIL through the trees. In just three minutes you reach the **Artemis trail**. Turn left; the trail crosses the runs of TWO SKI-LIFTS and gains a little height. Soon after the second lift there are some striking views across to the Turkish-occupied zone and west to the coast above Pafos.

At around **3h** you should reach the secondary road leading to the summit, opposite the INFORMATION BOARD marking the start of the Artemis trail (Alternative walk). All those for the 'golf balls' turn right and follow the road for about 1.5km/1mi to the TOP OF **Mount Olympus**, passing the Cyprus Ski Club café (only open in the skiing season), and returning to this spot after viewing.

The Artemis trail is another, slightly shorter (7km) circuit of Mount Olympus, not vastly different from the one just completed, but higher and a touch more dramatic. Save this for another day, *or* combine the two trails for a good long ramble. For the main walk, start out along Artemis, but then take the broad track that heads off to the left near trail point No 5. Then, after about 450m/yds, go left on a rocky track; it curves back north to rejoin the **Atalante trail** between points 9 and 10. Turn left again, and you should be back at **Troodos** at **4h** or sooner, after a splendid introduction to Mount Olympus. There are spectacular views at any time of year, with richly coloured flora in spring, and you will have barely climbed a hill all day. But do take a woollie. Snow can lie here after Easter!

Troodos in snow — very pretty, but make sure you don't try to follow any of the trails if the powder is still deep!

2 TROODOS • MAKRYA KONTARKA • TROODOS

See map pages 54-55; see photographs on pages 2 and 56

Distance: 6km/4mi; 1h35min   **Grade**: easy; almost level walking

Equipment: stout shoes, sunhat, water, picnic; fleece and waterproof in winter

How to get there and return: as Walk 1, page 49

Alternative walk: Troodos — Caledonian Falls — Platres (12km/7.4mi; 3h40min; fairly easy descent of 600m/1970ft). At the crossroads reached in 35min, turn right and follow an easy, rough forestry road for about 5km to Kryos Potamos (info board), where you can pick up Walk 3. Or link up with Walk 5; there are endless permutations!

This splendid, easy stroll packs a wide variety of scenery into a short distance. It's a lovely way of getting some Troodos air after a drive up from Lemesos.

Start out by walking south along **Troodos** main street. Pass the TROODOS HOTEL on the left and go up the road signed to the police station. Pass a CTO INFORMATION BOARD, and as the road bends sharp right, the Civic Restaurant (on your left). Some 25m/yds further on (opposite the POLICE STATION), fork left on the **Persephone nature trail**. In about **15min** come to the particularly attractive stand of tall pine trees and cluster of benches shown on page 56 (Picnic 2).

You don't need a rest yet, so keep going and at **23min** reach an obvious viewpoint. Look back the way you have come and enjoy a fine view of Mount Olympus — its old name is Khionistra. Then look ahead: to the left see the unmistakeable landmark of the Pano Amiandos asbestos mine, with the road to Kakopetria, Galata and Lefkosia just to its left. Should you travel that road during your stay, you will get an entirely different view of Pano Amiandos from the other side. It is a mighty excavation!

Turn left on a track (**29min**; about 30m before a 2km sign on the left). Come at **35min** to a CROSSROADS, where Psilon Dhendron is signposted to the right (Alternative walk); keep ahead here, and at **45min** you will be enjoying a spectacular panorama. This area, known as **Makrya Kontarka** (Picnic 2), is some 1680m/5510ft above sea level and affords breathtaking views of Pano Amiandos, Trimiklini and Saittas villages, the peaks of Kionia and Kakomallis … not to mention Lemesos harbour and Salt Lake, plus countless village vineyards. Plenty of seats are provided here, an ideal place to settle down with flask and sandwiches, or my idea of a good picnic — a stick of *soujoukko* and a nip of Cyprus brandy!

Return to **Troodos** the same way (**1h35min**).

3 TROODOS • CALEDONIAN FALLS • PLATRES

See map pages 54-55; see also photographs pages 2, 51, 56

Distance: 4km/2.5mi; 1h35min

Grade: quite easy descent of about 450m/1475ft, but beware of turned ankles where the stony path twists and turns.

Equipment: stout shoes, sunhat, water, picnic; fleece and waterproof in winter

How to get there and return: as Walk 1, page 49. From Platres take a taxi to Kryos Potamos or Troodos to start the walk.

Alternative walks: 1) Begin the walk in Troodos itself; you can reach the start after a pleasant 2km walk by following the quiet old zigzagging road that leads off the Platres road opposite the signpost to the Dolphin Restaurant. 2) See Alternative walk 2 opposite.

The nature trail on which this walk is based is a mere 2km long — even shorter than Walk 2. But the going is somewhat harder because of twists and turns in the path and stepping stones which criss-cross the stream many times as you make your way to the falls.

The walk starts about 1.5KM SOUTH OF **Troodos** on the main road to Platres, opposite a sign indicating the KRYOS POTAMOS ('Cold River') and the CALEDONIAN FALLS. Follow the small road for about 500m, to a CTO INFORMATION BOARD below the President's summer cottage. Take the path to the right. Now stop and listen … for if it's high summer you may be hearing your first babbling brook of the holiday. Many streams dry up in summer, but not the **Kryos Potamos**. At about **6min** look out on the right for the first of numerous stream crossings. At **15min** a series of wooden steps cut into the hillside achieves a descent of about 20m/65ft in a short distance. They are steep, so take extra care in wet weather.

Nimble walkers might reach the **Caledonian Falls** (Picnic 3) in **35min**. But those of us peering at all the points of interest on the nature trail — and the less fleet of foot — might take around **45min**. Stay on the downhill path below the falls, following the stream. Half an hour later, the aroma of grilled trout heralds the TROUT FARM and restaurant (**Psilon Dhendron; 1h15min**). Cross the road and continue into **Platres** (**1h35min**).

Caledonian Falls (Picnic 3)

53

4 TROODOS • MAKRYA KONTARKA • MESAPOTAMOS MONASTERY • PLATRES

See map pages 54-55; see also photographs pages 2, 51

Distance: 16km/10mi; 4h

Grade: quite easy, but there is one steep, fairly strenuous descent on a gravelly path. Total descent just over 800m/2600ft; ascent about 200m/650ft. The end of the walk can be a bit of a slog in hot weather.

Equipment: boots or stout shoes, sunhat, water, picnic; fleece and waterproof in winter; optional trekking pole(s)

How to get there and return: As Walk 1, page 49. Take a taxi from Platres to Troodos to start.

Alternative walks: See Walks 2, 3 and 5.

Grand views await you on this easy-to-follow but longish ramble which takes in a vast opencast mine and a deserted monastery.

There are two ways of **starting the walk** at **Troodos**. In either case follow Walk 2 on page 52. About 100m short of the POLICE STATION you can take the track sign-

posted 'MESAPOTAMOS 13KM'. I prefer to keep along Walk 2, enjoying the **Persephone nature trail**. At the **35min**-point in that walk, turn left at the 'CROSSROADS' and join the above-mentioned track to Mesapotamos, which can be stony underfoot at times.

From here there are closer views of the PANO AMIANDOS MINE — the largest opencast asbestos mine in the world. Is it an eyesore or part of the landscape? Form your own judgment. At about **1h**, during which time the mine has dominated the view, it suddenly disap-

'Golf balls' at the radar installations (top) are a Troodos landmark; benches on the Persephone nature trail (Picnic 2)

Cyprus lacemakers (top) and the ruined Mesapotamos Monastery (Picnic 4)

pears from sight, as the track turns sharply right, twice. Those who have done Walk 2 will recognise, but be closer to, the vast panorama away to the left.

The track falls away sharply to the left for a short time, but after about 250m/yds, you can take a descending path to the left, on a gentler incline. Keep straight down this forest path (ignore any crossing paths or tracks). At first the descent is very steep (and sometimes slippery with rubble), but about halfway down an easier track comes underfoot. It takes you to a wider track, where a signpost indicates 'PLATRES 7KM' to the right. You'll return to this signpost after visiting the old monastery, which is a short walk to the left.

Mesapotamos Monastery (**2h**; Picnic 4) is in a wooded valley, helpfully cooler than the various tracks that lead to it, and you'll find there a welcoming stream of drinking water. But there are no other facilities: make sure you've brought a picnic! There is an official site nearby and another 10 minutes further west by the Arkolahania Stream (with barbecues, drinking water and toilets), if you like those sort of places. I'd rather find shade under a tree.

Return to the aforementioned signpost. The track rises some 200m over 4km. Beyond a signpost ('PLATRES 3KM'), it's a pleasant stroll to the TROUT FARM (**Psilon Dhendron**) and **Platres** itself, reached at about **4h**, depending on the heat and the feet.

5 PSILON DHENDRON • POUZIARIS • PSILON DHENDRON

See map pages 54-55; see also photographs pages 2, 51, 53, 56

Distance: 9.5km/6mi; 2h30min

Grade: moderate, with an ascent/descent of 400m/1300ft; good paths throughout

Equipment: stout shoes, sunhat, water, picnic; fleece and waterproof in winter

How to get there and return: as Walk 1, page 49. Park near (or, from Platres, walk to) the trout farm at Psilon Dhendron and go up to the Pouziaris nature trail board.

Alternative walk: Psilon Dhendron — Kryos Potamos — Caledonian Falls — Psilon Dhendron (10km/6.2mi; 2h55min; moderate, with an ascent/descent of about 400m/1300ft, sometimes on stony paths; access and equipment as main walk). Follow the main walk to the 50min-point. Take the path straight ahead and reach the rough forest road linking the Persephone trail to Caledonian Falls trail (1h05min). Turn left and, from the Kryos Potamos shelter (1h20min), follow Walk 3 back to Psilon Dhendron (2h55min).

This is a wonderful circuit, with plenty to interest the nature lover and some marvellous views from the highest point. The ascent route follows an ancient mule trail, and the lovely woodland paths are full of bird life.

Start out by climbing the path to the left of the POUZIARIS NATURE TRAIL BOARD. It winds right and rises steadily through shady pines and junipers. As you bend left, notice the bench off to the right at a viewpoint (**6min**, Picnic 5) and a few strawberry trees, providing food for birds rather than for you! You'll see lots more later. Cross a forestry road, going slightly left (**11min**) and, at a junction with a sign to 'Psilon Dhendron 1km' (**16min**), turn left (the other path is your return route). Now on a wide old MULE TRAIL, you enjoy magnificent views back over Lemesos and Platres.

Cross another forest road, again going slightly left (**22min**), and reach a welcome bench overlooking the Kryos Valley (**40min**). Round the slopes, with steep drops to the left, and cross the bed of a stream (often dry). Almost immediately, turn right uphill (**50min**). *(But for the Alternative walk take the path straight ahead.)* The woodland path rises to a bench and a tall iron pylon with a huge flat grey board. This is the SUMMIT of **Pouziaris** (**1h03min**) — not really a peak, just a plateau. After taking in the superb views over the south coast and puzzling over the purpose of the 'signal tower', continue to a junction 50m/yds further on, where there are two signs, both indicating Psilon Dhendron (**1h06min**). Take the path to the right, downhill ('PSILON DHENDRON 6KM').

58

Above: strawberry trees (Arbutus unedo) abound on this walk; right: the old mule trail above the Kryos River

Your path now undulates gently around this plateau and then begins to zigzag down with a few steep stony sections. When you meet a track at a bench (**1h28min**), cross over and pick up the path on the other side. Soon you meet the track again; this time follow it downhill to the right, through mixed pines interspersed with more strawberry trees. Where the track makes a sharp bend to the right, *ignore* a path to the left signed to Psilon Dhendron; it goes down to the forestry road of Walk 4 and is a much longer route home! Your track, still signed to Psilon Dhendron, soon crosses a forestry road (**1h35min**). Beyond a stream bed, go straight ahead on a rocky downhill stretch. This is followed by a level, smooth section with pine needles cushioning your aching feet, and then a long, but gentle ascent. You will wonder if you are heading back to Troodos as you continue gently climbing, but worry not — the end is not too far away. Several rockfalls are easily negotiated, as you reach a welcome bench with views to Platres (**2h05min**).

The path continues, winding right and descending quite sharply to meet a track at the foot of a few steps (**2h13min**). Cross the track, heading slightly right, and pick up your onward path again. Continue down to meet the old MULE TRAIL coming in from the right (**2h16min**). Having rejoined your outgoing route, you'll soon hear the welcome sound of running water from the trout farm and come to **Psilon Dhendron** (**2h30min**).

6 TROODITISSA

See map pages 54-55   **Distance**: 10km/6.2mi; 2h45min

Grade: easy, with one uphill stretch of 2.5km (just over 150m/490ft)

Equipment: walking boots or stout shoes, sunhat, water, picnic; fleece and waterproof in winter

How to get there and return: as Walk 1, page 49. To both start and end the walk, use a taxi from Platres to Trooditissa and be sure to arrange a return pick-up, allowing enough time to enjoy the walk.

Shorter walk: Trooditissa Monastery — Kambi tou Kaloyerou (5.5km/ 3.4mi; 1h30min; grade and access as above). Arrange with the Platres taxi driver to collect you at the Kambi tou Kaloyerou picnic site on the Prodhromos road (E804) — but you will not have escaped the climb!

Trooditissa Monastery, nestling in the Troodos Mountains some 5km northwest of Platres, was founded in 1250, and among its treasures are ancient icons and a leather belt decorated with silver medallions. Tradition has it that wearing the belt promotes fertility in women. Until quite recently, one of the monks would happily produce this potent object for visitors, but perhaps because of increasing tourism, the monastery is now only open to Cypriots. That does not, however, detract from the appeal of this most scenic walk.

The walk starts at **Trooditissa**, about 50 metres beyond the monastery entrance, where a signpost indicates 'AYIOS DHIMITRIOS 9KM'. That is not our destination, but it is the track to follow. It soon curves round to the southwest, offering magnificent views over Phini village in the valley far below. At **20min** reach another track leading off to the right, but ignore it; you will recognise this junction on the way back — it's the return route. Continue down to the left, and in **25min** you'll see a signpost indicating Phini 4km. Ignore this too!

At **50min**, at a clearing with a ROUND WATER TANK, a signpost indicates Ayios Dhimitrios straight ahead, but we turn right, for a gentle climb of 2.5km to the Prodhromos road. This section of the walk is not in the 'brutal' category, but it can be a bit of a sweat in hot weather. Stop for a breather occasionally and puzzle over the inviting-looking tracks that lead downhill, but ignore them all. Keep on uphill to the TROODITISSA/ PRODHROMOS ROAD (**1h30min**). The **Kambi tou Kaloyerou** picnic site across the road is a pleasant location, with tables and benches among the tall trees, barbecues and a play area for young children. This is an excellent place to take a break, or end the walk if you have a pick-up arranged.

Leaving the picnic site, turn left along the road towards Trooditissa, and follow it for some 10 minutes,

View to Phini from the Trooditissa track. Phini has a museum and a pottery of some note. Right: rock rose (Cistus parviflorus, top) and cress (Arabis purpurea)

ignoring the first track you see off to the right. In about **1h40min** you'll come to a sharp right turn in the road. Stop, and locate a track that leads off the road to the right, close to a pair of CONCRETE WATER TANKS (there is a signpost, 'TROODITISSA 3KM', in the curve of the road here). You now follow this track all the way back to the junction first encountered 20 minutes from the start of the walk. In its early stages, this track may show evidence of rockfalls; it is liberally strewn with rocks and boulders. The risk of further falls is greater after heavy rain, and it's possible that you will have to return to the road and follow this to Trooditissa, should you be walking in winter or early spring.

The track is really a high-level version of the outward journey and offers spectacular views to the south and west. At around **2h25min** reach the junction first passed 20min into the walk; turn left and in **2h45min** you should be back at **Trooditissa**, where a café opens in summer and on *some weekends* in winter.

7 MADHARI RIDGE

Distance: 7.5km/4.7mi, 2h30min; optional extra 3.5km (1h) round Mount Adelphi

Grade: moderate climb of under 300m/980ft; some short, steep stretches

Equipment: walking boots or stout shoes, sunhat, water, picnic; fleece and waterproof in winter

How to get there and return: 🚗 by car, leave Troodos on the Lefkosia road (B9). Beyond Pano Amiandos, turn off right for Kyperounda. After about 4km, turn left towards 'Spilia 5km'. Park 1.8km along, at Doxasi o Theos, where there is an information board on the right.

Alternative walks: The *approximate* routes of two other CTO nature trails are highlighted on the map below *in yellow*. One leads from the starting point for the main walk along Madhari Ridge, turns north to Selladi tou Karamanli, west to Moulti tis Choras, and back to Doxasi o Theos. Total distance 13km/8mi; about 4h30min-5h, with climbs/descents of about 500m/1640ft overall. The other runs between two charming Byzantine churches — Stavros tou Agiasmati (a detour off the Peristerona road) and Panayia tou Araka near Lagoudhera. This out-and-back walk is 15km/9.3mi; 5h, with ascents of 600m/2000ft. To halve the distance/ascent, leave your car in Lagoudhera. You should be able to call a taxi from one of the coffee houses, to take you to Stavros tou Agiasmati. Walk from there back to your car.

Mount Adelphi is the second highest point on Cyprus (1613m/5290ft), and this walk to it along an exposed ridge is even more spectacular than the approach to Mount Olympus. It can be strenuous for short

stretches, and the track stony, but the views are stunning — from the northern, Turkish side of the island to the south, where Kyperounda clings to the opposite hillside like magic.

Start out at the INFORMATION BOARD for the **Doxasi o**

Kyperounda from Madhari Ridge (Picnic 7)

Theos ('Glory to God') nature trail: climb sharply to the right and, when you come to a fork where you can go ahead or left, keep left. You soon reach a rocky outcrop with a wonderful view northwards towards Morphou Bay. At around **15min** come to a bench (Picnic 7) from where there are equally breathtaking views over Kyperounda and towards the Pano Amiandos mine and the 'golf balls' on Mount Olympus.

Walk the trail through pine trees, and at around **40min** drop down to a small clearing with views over the Mesaoria Plain and towards Mount Adelphi — another setting for Picnic 7. This could mark the end of a short version of this walk if you didn't fancy the climb ahead. But it isn't as bad as it looks, honestly! It can be quite cool and breezy on top, even in summer.

Skip up to the TOP OF **Madhari Ridge** (**50min**) like a moufflon, and you'll be rewarded with wonderful views! Turn left and walk along the ridge, taking the air, and lots of photographs. You'll see Kyperounda again to your right, and Chandria with its striking modern church. Reservoirs glimmer between the two villages.

White cairns indicate viewpoints to your left (climb slightly to reach them), then **Mount Adelphi** with the FIREWATCH POINT at its peak comes into view. Climb the last stretch for some truly magnificent views and, if you wish, do the extra signposted 'Teisia tis Madaris' circuit (add one hour). The fire-watcher usually spends a three-day shift up here — rather a lonely existence. If he isn't busy, he'll be delighted to spend some time with you.

Then retrace your steps to the **Doxasi o Theos** INFOR-MATION BOARD (**2h30min**). If you haven't been impressed by the views from the ridge, the brandy sours are on me if we ever meet!

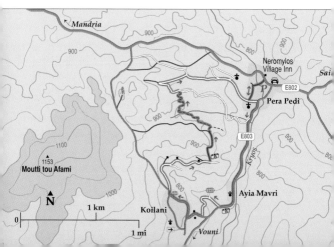

8 PERA PEDI • AYIA MAVRI • KOILANI • PERA PEDI

See map opposite   **Distance:** 7.5km/4.7mi; 2h10min

Grade: moderate, with some steep climbing on good roads or tracks and a tricky descent on a loose-stoned path. Ascent/descent 250m/820ft

Equipment: walking boots, sunhat, water, optional picnic; trekking pole(s), long trousers for the steep path descent through prickly bushes.

How to get there and return: 🚗 to Pera Pedi (the 56km-point in Car tour 4). Park in the car park and make your way to Neromylos Village Inn on the main street. Or 🚐 to Platres and taxi (as Walk 1, page 49)

Short walks

1 Ayia Mavri (3km/1.9mi; 52min; easy — trainers will suffice). Follow the main walk to Ayia Mavri (restaurants) and return the same way.

2 Ayia Mavri and Koilani. (5km/3mi; 1h30min; moderate, but trainers will suffice). Follow the main walk to the 45min-point, explore the fascinating (but steep) streets of the village and visit its museums. Return the same way. Allow ample time for exploration.

T he three villages featured on this walk are very different; each has its own unique character, and all are delightful. Their livelihood comes from the vineyards you will pass en route and, if you have time, you can visit Koilani's wine museum and sample the produce in any number of local tavernas.

Start the walk at the NEROMYLOS VILLAGE INN. Opposite, just to the left, is a crazy-paved pedestrian lane. Follow it over a bridge across the permanently running **Kryos River** (**1min**; Picnic 8). After it becomes a track, turn left at a T-junction and left again at the CHURCH (**5min**). The track rises, then falls to meet the narrow road to Ayia Mavri and Vouni (**10min**), where you turn right. From here you'll be on tarmac for some time, but it makes for easy walking and there is plenty of interest along the way. The road runs alongside the river and through the gorge, past a fairytale cottage on the opposite bank. **Ayia Mavri** (**26min**) is a small hamlet with several restaurants and a little church. *(Short walk 1 turns back here.)*

Continue, now rising, with superb views over left to fertile terraces. Turn right on a roughly surfaced road, signposted to Koilani in Greek (**33min**). Still climbing, wind through vineyards. Turn right when you reach a tarmac road (**41min**) and soon pass the AYIA MAVRI WINERY at the entrance to **Koilani** village (**45min**). *(After exploring the village, Short walk 2 returns the same way.)*

Walk up through this fascinating village, keeping right at all forks. You pass TAVERNA STREET on your left (**50min**) — if you have time, detour along it to visit its museums. At a junction with two exit ('Exodus') signs, go right and

Winery at Ayia Mavri, vines and gourds

pass a BASKETBALL PITCH. This is AFAMI STREET (named for the 1153m peak to the west). As you leave the old village, with only a couple of new houses ahead, take a track on the right (PANAGIAS AGIASMATOS; **59min**). Head down past some noisy, but chained or caged dogs. Follow this track, going left at a fork, to pass below some animal shelters with more dogs, guarding the vines on the right.

Ignore a track going back to the left and head first downhill, then up to a fork (**1h11min**). Your route is the steeply rising track to the left. If you've been sampling the local grape, you'll hardly skip up here like a moufflon — so take it a few steps at a time, pausing to look back over Koilani. Finally you reach a level stretch (**1h21min**) which takes you round the top of four vine terraces. Then, on a sharp left-hand bend, look for a clear path of loose stones down to the right, marked by a CAIRN (**1h24min**). It's steep and a bit of a scramble in places, so *take care.* Look for CAIRNS marking junctions, particularly the first one, after only 20 metres, where you must go sharp left — ignoring the path going straight ahead towards a cliff. Pass between prickly bushes, and locate in the distance a small grassy terrace on the opposite side of the narrow valley. Your path wends its way to the VALLEY FLOOR (**1h36min**) and rises again through the GRASSY TERRACE — the mirror image of your descent path. Reach the top (**1h43min**), and notice the wide track below you, with Pera Pedi beyond. Follow the path down left and scramble to the track (**1h50min**).

Turn left along the track and meet another track (1ST APRIL STREET; **2h**). Turn right, noticing a large church over to the left. Continue ahead without deviation to AGIOU NIKOLAOU STREET and wind down left to the CHURCH passed on your outward route. Go back past the riverside picnic spot, to the main road in **Pera Pedi (2h10min)**.

9 STAVROS TIS PSOKAS

Distance: 13.5km/8.4mi; 4h

Grade: fairly strenuous, with ascents of about 550m/1800ft overall; some gravelly surfaces underfoot

Equipment: stout shoes or walking boots, sunhat, water, picnic; fleece and waterproof in winter. Trekking poles are useful for the gravelly descents.

How to get there and return: 🚗 by car from Pafos via Kannaviou; from Polis via Lyso; from Troodos via Kykko Monastery. *NB: In winter and early spring, access (by track) from*

Forestry station at Stavros

Pafos may only be possible in a 4WD vehicle; the routes via Kykko and Lyso are asphalted. Park just over 1km outside Stavros on the Kykko road, as close as possible to the Horteri nature trail information board (on the right). Or park at Stavros and start the circuit there.

Short walks

1 **Horteri nature trail** (5km/3mi, 1h30min; moderate, with an initial ascent of about 250m/820ft) and a steep descent. Park at the nature trail board and follow the main walk for 1h30min.

2 **Selladi tou Stavrou nature trail** (2.5km/1.6mi; 45min; easy). Park at Selladi tou Stavrou junction, where there is a nature trail shelter/information board. Pick up the main walk at the 2h10min-point, leave it at the afforestation sign and return to your car.

The Forestry Department runs a forest station at Stavros, where there is also a small café and very popular hostel accommodation (see page 44). To encourage intimate acquaintance with the environment, the department has also created three nature trails around Stavros, and information about the area is available from the forestry office. Take time, too, to visit the moufflon enclosure just north of the forestry office. This rare Cyprus sheep — which was once almost extinct — is a very shy creature, so chances of spotting it in the wild are rare! Since the Stavros nature trails are not adjacent, my 'grand tour' takes in short stretches of road-walking and could be quite tiring on a warm day. A much easier option is to do the two Short walks as separate circuits.

Begin at the **Horteri trail** SHELTER/INFORMATION BOARD (by a SPRING). Keep ahead at a fork two minutes up (you will return on the path to the left). The path rises gently but steadily through strongly scented pines. Excellent views over the whole valley setting of Stavros and to the fire-watch point on Horteri are your reward for reaching trail point No 16. Continue uphill to a fork and benches at point No 22 (**50min**), where you keep left on the nature trail. (Heading right you could climb to the top of Horteri

67

for even wider-ranging views over the Akamas Peninsula; allow 45 minutes extra for this diversion.) After a fairly steep descent, the trail descends to the HORTERI TRAIL SHELTER (**1h30min**).

From here follow the asphalt road north, to **Selladi tou Stavrou** (**2h10min**), a major junction where two signposted trails begin ('softies' can drive here, to start Short walk 2). Climb the steps up to a fork and keep right (Short walk 2 will return to this point after completing a loop). Soon, from a plateau, there is a fine view reaching west to the Akamas Peninsula. Later, a lovely stretch along a north/south ridge affords more magnificent views. You will come to a sign indicating that reafforestation is in progress on the opposite hillside (see photograph caption on page 70). (Here Short walk 2 heads sharp left to complete the circuit.) The main walk turns right, zigzagging southwest down the ridge. The surface underfoot is rather loose with rubble, so take care. The views all around are superb, and you should spot a seat at which a sign proclaims 'nice view of the Stavros valley'… with which there can be no argument.

The trail descends to a track by a helipad (**3h15min**), where you turn left to **Stavros** (**3h30min**). From here walk up the Kykko road back to your car at the **Horteri trail** (**4h**).

10 CEDAR VALLEY AND MOUNT TRIPYLOS

Distance: 14km/8.7mi, 4h

Grade: quite easy, with an ascent of about 250m/820ft; all on forestry roads and tracks. If possible, set out early; there may be heavy 4WD traffic in Cedar Valley en route to the picnic area or Kykko.

Equipment: walking boots or stout shoes, sunhat, water, picnic; fleece and waterproof in winter

How to get there and return: 🚗 by car from Troodos via Kykko Monastery, from Pafos via Kannaviou and Stavros, or from from Polis via Lyso and Stavros. *NB: In winter and early spring, access (by track) from Pafos may only be possible in a 4WD vehicle; the routes via Kykko and Lyso are asphalted.* Park at the Dhodheka Anemi junction (8km southeast of Stavros on the Kykko road); there is a sign here, 'Cedar Valley 10km'.

Short walk: Mount Tripylos (4km/2.5mi; 1h15min; grade as above). At the junction you will see a gated track (from which vehicles are barred) signposted to Mount Tripylos. Park here and simply follow the track uphill for 2km and return the same way.

Whether you make this walk your prime target for the day, or choose the shorter version while on a trip to Kykko, you are sure to enjoy it! The views are splendid, and the surroundings beautiful. The longer (main) walk is easy to follow, largely on shaded Cyprus earthen roads among fragrant pines and towering cedars.

Begin at the **Dhodheka Anemi** JUNCTION: follow the road signposted 'Cedar Valley 10km'. It *is* technically an unsurfaced road (although only suitable for 4WD), but in reality it makes a beautiful, easy-surfaced walk, gently downwards at this stage, through open pine woods.

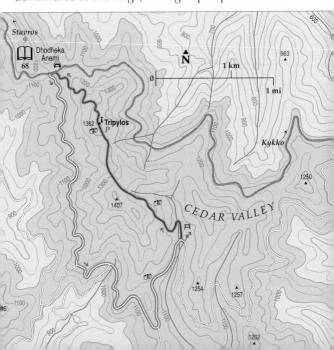

The forests around Stavros and Cedar Valley are in a healthier state now than they were in the early 1900s, and Winston Churchill can be credited for improving matters after 1907 when, as Under Secretary of State for the Colonies, he allocated funds for extensive tree-planting. The forests flourished in the ensuing years, but their welfare was not aided by the invading Turkish forces: in 1974 their air force needlessly set fire to over 150 square kilometres of trees. Recovery is continuing, thanks to the work of the Forestry Department.

You will pass three roads that head off to the right, and will experience stunning views to the south and west as your way curves gradually round to the east. After about **2h**, cedars will appear among the pine trees and become much more evident as you reach the area that gave rise to the name of **Cedar Valley**. You will come to a small PICNIC AREA with a water supply, close to a group of plane trees (**2h30min**).

The route now leaves the main valley road, and gently climbs a forestry track up the slopes of Mount Tripylos for 2.5km, with views opening out all around. If you are to see moufflon in the wild on your trip to Cyprus, this could be the day! Cedar trees are still very much in evidence as you approach the SUMMIT OF **Mount Tripylos** (**3h30min**). From this peak (1362m/4470ft) there are magnificent views — eastward to Troodos, westward to the Akamas, and north to Morphou Bay. At the top you'll see a fire-watch station and a small picnic area which couldn't have a more lovely setting (Picnic 10)!

From here it's a simple stroll of 2km back to **Dhodheka Anemi** and your car, reached in around **4h**. On a clear day the air could not have been fresher, nor the views more appealing.

11 CIRCUIT FROM AYIOS NEOPHYTOS

Distance: 8km/5mi, 1h50min

Grade: moderate, with a steep initial ascent, a steep final descent, and some overgrown paths. Ascent/descent about 250m/820ft overall.

Equipment: walking boots or stout shoes, sunhat, water, long trousers; optional trekking pole(s)

How to get there and return: 🚗 car or taxi to/from Ayios Neophytos. Or 🚌 from Pafos (Tala bus, Timetable E9, stops at Ayios Neophytos); return on the same bus from Tala (2km away). Or Pafos-Polis 🚌 (Timetable E5) to Tsadha, from where you can walk 1km and join the walk at the 1h-point and circle back to the same point.

The 12th-century monastery of St Neophytos is about 10km north of Pafos and dedicated to a man who was a noted scholar and writer, devoted man of God, and a hermit who chose a life of reclusion in caves that can still be seen by visitors. Some have beautiful frescoes that can be closely inspected, whether on a car outing or as a prelude to this circuit of the monastery valley.

Start out from the PLATANOS SNACK BAR at **Ayios Neophytos** by walking back towards Pafos and *past* the turning for Tala. Some 650m/yds from the snack bar, look out for an old stone warehouse with recent extension, and 50m/yds before it, turn sharp left on a chained-off farm track. This climbs steeply through vineyards (**5min**), but the effort is rewarded with ever-improving views over the monastery. Ignore a track off left, and another right. Turn sharp left to round an olive grove, then turn left uphill on a wide track (**15min**). You touch briefly on a surfaced road, then head left on a track below the summit of **Melissovounos**. Continue steadily uphill towards the radio aerials. (If you wish, take a detour of 300m/yds to the top, to gain views towards Pafos and the coast.)

Otherwise, bear left (**45min**) and follow the track along the crest of a hill, gently undulating, and sur-

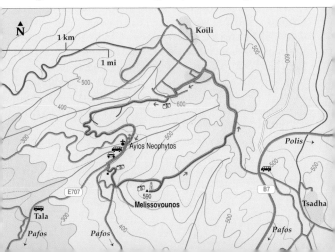

Wall painting at Ayios Neophytos and the monastery courtyard

rounded by vineyards. You come to a quiet road (**1h**), where you turn left towards the village of Koili. After about 1km you will pass two signs to **Koili** (opposite the second sign there is a bus shelter). A few metres/yards beyond this second sign, turn left. This road goes through a housing estate and after about 50m/yds bears right. At a T-junction, go left, then turn right on MAKADONIAS STREET.

After 30m/yds turn left downhill on a concrete track through vineyards (**1h 20min**), enjoying splendid views towards the distant coast. The concrete soon changes to dirt, and you'll see the masts ahead on Melissovounos. Ignore a track off right and one off left at a short concrete section. At a major fork, take the track going slightly right. Ignore a stony track going sharply downhill to the right and take the next track to the right (just before a HUNTING SIGN; **1h30min**). Keep winding downhill. When you see the monastery directly below you, the track ends. From here an indistinct, overgrown path leads in a couple of minutes to a much clearer, rocky path. Follow this down to the large WATER TANK at **Ayios Neophytos** (**1h50min**).

12 AROUND KATHIKAS

See photographs page 25

Distance: 7.5km/4.7mi; 1h50min

Grade: easy (ascents of only 100m/300ft)

Equipment: walking boots or stout shoes, sunhat, water, picnic

How to get there and return: 🚗 car to/from Kathikas

Short walk: Agiasmata nature trail (3.5km/2.2mi; 1h; easy). Follow the main walk for 45min, then turn left to Kathikas.

Alternative walk: Akoursos (10km/6mi; 3h; easy, but with a stiff climb 280m/920ft back from Akoursos. Follow the main walk to the 1h08min-point, then detour to Akoursos, a very old community with a disused mosque, an old olive press ... and a spooky cemetery.

This walk, in an area developed by the Laona Project (see page 22) gives stunning views down a ravine full of jackdaws to the coast at Coral Bay. We then walk through vineyards, flushing partridge by the score.

Start from the LAONA VISITOR CENTRE beside the CHURCH in **Kathikas**. Walk south down the Akoursos road and after 300m/yds turn right on AGIASMATOS STREET. This street soon bears left and becomes concrete. Turn right on the signposted **Agiasmata nature trail** (**15min**). The rocky path descends past a turning to the 'official' start of the trail and comes to a bench at a SPRING (**20min**; Picnic 12). Take the path to the right, cross the ravine and ascend under the cliffs, before contouring along the edge for a short way. Turn left on a track and, at the next sign, turn left and zigzag up to another bench (**39min**), with a fine view to distant Coral Bay. Continue to a dirt road and turn left to a crossroads (**45min**).

Turn right *(left for the Short walk)* and pass the front of the not-very-ancient chapel of **Ayia Marina**, then stroll on to a three-way junction (**1h01min**). Go left, and at the signposted crossroads turn left on the narrow Kathikas road (**1h08min**) — or first detour right to Akoursos *(Alternative walk)*. Descend to a long row of beehives and, about 200m/yds after the road begins to climb again, turn right on a clear track down into fields (**1h21min**). Follow this to another track at a tin hut. Turn left; you will see Kathikas ahead. As your track veers sharp right towards a pink house, go left on a narrower track (**1h33min**). Wind up past a lone cypress tree and reach the road again (**1h40min**). Turn right, back to **Kathikas** (**1h50min**).

13 KISSONERGA TO CORAL BAY

Distance: 8.5km/5.3mi, 2h30min

Grade: easy, ascents of only 100m/330ft

Equipment: stout shoes, sunhat, water, picnic, swimming things

How to get there: 🚗 car or taxi to Kissonerga; by car park near the sports ground near the church. Or 🚌 from Pafos (not in the timetables; check at the tourist office or with the Alepa Bus Co: see Timetable E7).
To return: 🚌 from Coral Bay to Pafos (Timetable E8), or to the junction of the Coral Bay/Kissonerga road, from where it is a 15min walk back to your car. Some buses return from Coral Bay to Pafos via Kissonerga (check at the tourist office or with the Alepa Bus Co: see Timetable E8).

In the 1990s this ramble to the main irrigation reservoir of the Pafos region was marred by the intrusion of a military camp. But, perhaps because it is so close to Pafos and so easy, it remains popular with 'Landscapers'.

The walk starts at **Kissonerga**, a village which straddles the road between Pafos centre and Coral Bay. Cross the SPORTS PITCH beside the church, then cross the main road. Head up APIS STREET; you pass the village CEMETERY, on your left, after about 100m/yds. Soon fork left and, at a T-junction (**15min**), turn left. You are now heading almost due north, walking past fruit and vegetable plots. Pass PADDOCKS RIDING STABLE on the left and notice the 'no photography' signs — there's a military base ahead.

About 1km beyond the T-junction, just coming out of a sharp Z-bend, turn left along a track, lined on the left with TALL CONIFERS (**30min**). You will soon reach an area with a small fenced-off WATER CONTROL POINT and a junction of tracks. Here your track swings right and follows a concrete WATER CHANNEL on the right (initially covered with concrete slabs). Follow this watercourse, with fine views over citrus groves as it heads inland.

At **50min** notice the cultivation below to your left and ignore a track to the right as you skirt orange groves. Pass a large gate just off to the right, bearing the notice 'Idiotikos Dromos, Private Road', as you bear left along a fence and zigzag down through orange trees to the bottom of the valley, where a ruined building is opposite. Turn left through the citrus trees, away from the dam. After 300m/yds join a rough road and turn right uphill, climbing gently to the **Mavrokolymbos Dam** (Picnic 13; **1h15min**). Have a look at the steps, the sluice, a ruined building and an old bridge. A fine excuse for a breather!

Follow the track past the dam wall, and almost certainly see sheep and goats near the water's edge. About 500m/yds beyond the dam wall, at **1h20min**, turn sharp

left on a track and climb to the AKOURSOS ROAD (**1h35min**). Turn left: it's downhill almost all the way (4km) to **Coral Bay** (**2h30min**), where you can take a dip. Or flag down a bus as soon as you reach the busy coast road.

Above: citrus groves flourish in the valley below the Mavrokolymbos Dam. The dam is a key part of the irrigation system for the agricultural industry around Pafos. Below: Coral Bay

14 LARA BEACH

See map and photographs on pages 78-79

Distance: 3km/2mi; 1h   **Grade**: easy

Equipment: stout shoes, sunhat, water, picnic, swimming things

How to get there and return: 🚗 car to/from Lara Beach, 27km north of Pafos via Coral Bay. The road is asphalted as far as a U-bend at the Aspros River; it then reverts to a wide unsurfaced road. Just 1.1km further on you'll see the signposted track to the Avagas Gorge on the right (Walk 16). After about 4km, beyond a sign to Lara Restaurant, the last 1km of track is very eroded — best done in a 4WD vehicle (or walked). Or 🚢 from Pafos (check at the tourist office for times)

Alternative walk: Avagas Gorge and Lara Beach (17km/10.5mi; 6h). Quite easy, but long. Park at the mouth of the Aspros River just north of Cape Drepanon (where the asphalt runs out). Walk into the Avagas Gorge (see Walk 16) and then on to Lara for this circuit. A great day out; worth putting the boots on!

Special note: Access may be restricted in July-August during the nesting season of the rare green turtle. Please observe relevant warning signs.

This attractive, unspoiled beach, setting for Picnic 14, can only be reached by car, or perhaps on a sea cruise out of Pafos during summer. By car it is a leisurely drive north, passing close to Coral Bay, then Ayios Yeoryios. (A short detour here will show you an attractive fishing refuge and interesting church overlooking the sea.) The whole area dates back to Roman times and has been the scene of much excavation.

Thankfully, Lara has been spared the ravages of commerce; one can tolerate and even give thanks for the single seasonal restaurant near the beach which caters for most of Lara's visitors. Apart from the restaurant, there's absolutely nothing at Lara except wonderful coastal scenery and a quiet atmosphere. A most agreeable stroll can be made along and around the beach for an hour or two.

Start out near the LARA RESTAURANT at **Lara Beach**, walking down to the shoreline. At the north end of the beach is a headland crossed by tracks, offering very pleasing views south along the coast and inland to the hills north of Peyia. Close to Lara are the summer nesting grounds of the rare and protected green turtle.

North of Lara, the rough road gets even rougher before petering out after a few kilometres (see 4WD options for Car tour 1 on page 24), but there are some very secluded coves along here if you fancy skinny-dipping.

Thankfully, the Akamas Peninsula which includes the Lara region was made a national park area early in the 1990s, thus ensuring its continuing existence as a totally unspoiled, totally beautiful landscape.

15 FROM DROUSSEIA TO AYIOS YEORYIOS

See map pages 78-79; see photographs pages 78, 79, 80, 81
Distance: 18km/11.2mi; about 5h

Grade: fairly easy but long, with a descent of about 600m/2000ft

Equipment: walking boots or stout shoes, sunhat, plenty of water, picnic

How to get there: 🚌 to Polis (Timetable E5), then taxi to Drousseia (or with friends)
To return: 🚗 telephone for a taxi when you arrive at Ayios Yeoryios (or arrange for friends to meet you)

Alternative walks: Masochists can link up Walks 14 or 16 en route.

In the cooler months of spring and autumn it's most enjoyable to take a long Cyprus walk. This trek is quite easy, but choose a coolish day and carry plenty of water. There are no facilities of any kind on the route. The good news is that much of the walk is level or downhill (albeit on rough tracks), and the views over the whole Lara coastline will linger long in the memory.

Start out from **Drousseia**: follow *Alternative* walk 22 on page 96. When you reach the track (**28min**), turn right (past the modern church) and keep going until you come to the asphalted Androlikou–Kathikas road. Turn right here and, a short way along (just south of the ruined settlement of Pittikopos), turn left at a junction with a broad track (**50min**).

You now follow the roughest 'road' you're likely to find on Cyprus (4WD Option B in Car tour 1 bumps along here). After about 1km turn left, to start gaining views over the whole western coast around Lara Bay which is slightly to the left on the horizon. That is your target!

The way is simple, but don't rush it. Relish this *totally* unspoiled region, listen to the birdsong, smell the air, and take some wonderful photos as you follow the winding track gently downwards for some 7km, to join the rough road above **Lara**.

After visiting the beach (Walk 14), you have another 7km of walking on a similar road (past the turn-off to the **Avagas Gorge** and Walk 16). You should reach **Ayios Yeoryios** in under **5h**, depending on your stride, and how many times you stop to take in the scenery. You'll be tired and thirsty, but you'll thank me for this wonderful experience of the Akamas... but perhaps not immediately!

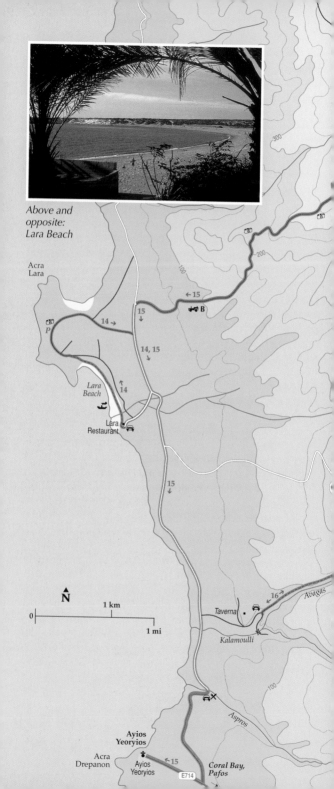

Above and opposite: Lara Beach

Acra
Lara

P

Lara
Beach

Lara
Restaurant

14 →

15 ↓

14, 15 ↓

↑ 14

← 15

B

15 ↓

N

0   1 km

         1 mi

Taverna

Kalamoulli

16 →

Avagas

Aspros

Ayios
Yeoryios

Acra
Drepanon

Ayios
Yeoryios

← 15

Coral Bay,
Pafos

E714

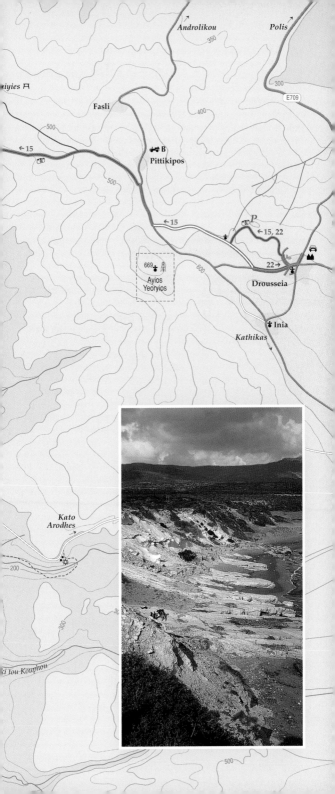

Androlikou

Polis

350

E709

300

Fasli

400

⟵ 15

500

500

B
Pittikipos

P

⟵ 15, 22

⟵ 15

669
Ayios
Yeoryios

600

22⟶

Drousseia

Inia

Kathikas

Kato
Arodhes

200

300

i Iou Kouphou

500

16 AVAGAS GORGE

See map and photographs on pages 78-79; see also cover photograph

Distance: 2km/1.2mi, 1h

Grade: quite easy, with some scrambling over boulders

Equipment: stout shoes (boots outside summer), sunhat, water, picnic

How to get there and return: 🚌 via Coral Bay and Ayios Yeoryios, 23km north of Pafos. Continue on track when the asphalt runs out 1.6km past Ayios Yeoryios, and turn right 1.1km further on at a signpost for the Avagas Gorge. You will soon see the Viklari Taverna up on the left. Drive down a track below and to the right of it. This drops down to a small parking place, where the track forks near two ravines.

From being almost a secret some years ago, the Avagas Gorge is now well visited, but it remains a dramatic geographical feature which deserves some respect. One of the best ways to enjoy the whole gorge is on a guided

trek with leaders who know the region intimately and will take you into the gorge from the top (photograph opposite). But it is easy enough to venture into the gorge from its mouth, walking only as far in as you feel comfortable.

Start out at the PARKING PLACE. Walk through a gate to the left, into the northerly and most spectacular of the two ravines, the **Avagas Gorge**. I suggest a foray of a mere 1km or so each way — this will let you see how its walls soar high above you and later narrow into a mighty passage, shutting out much of the sunlight (cover photograph. Outside summer there should be ample water, but in dry weather the flow is piped to nearby orchards.

If you get as far as thick undergrowth, be aware that snakes (see Walking: Nuisances) are not unknown here in very hot weather. After about half an hour, turn back when you've had enough. You may observe that some of the large boulders that you scramble round look newer than others... these came tumbling down the gorge walls in the most recent earthquake. Have a nice day!

Scenes of the Akamas: plateau above the Avagas Gorge (left); the abandoned village of Androlikou, now on the 'tourist route' (top); perils of not wearing a sunhat? (middle); fruit trees and wild flowers

81

17 KHAPOTAMI GORGE

Distance: 9.5km/6mi; 2h35min

Grade: moderate, with ascents of about 150m/500ft; it can be extremely hot in the gorge in high summer

Equipment: walking boots or stout shoes, sunhat, plenty of water, picnic

How to get there: 🚘 taxi from Pafos to Pano Arkhimandrita, shared to spread cost. It's a more expensive taxi journey from Lemesos.
To return: 🚘 pre-arranged taxi from Alekhtora, or take the village taxi to the main road at Pissouri, from where you could telephone for a service taxi bound for Pafos or Lemesos.

Circular walk for motorists: Kato Arkhimandrita — Khapotami Gorge — Kato Arkhimandrita (7.5km/4.7mi; 2h30min; grade as main walk; note that the ascent at the end of the walk is in full sun and to be avoided in summer). 🚘 car to Pano Arkhimandrita. After viewing the shrine, drive 2.5km on the rough road leading from the village water tanks, to park at Kato Arkhimandrita. Pick up the main walk at the 45min-point and follow it to just past the 2h05min-point. Then take the *second* track off to the left, with farm buildings and shelters on both sides. It's a long, steady climb up here, with no shade, so take it easy. You pass a pylon on the left, part-way up. Close to the top of the ridge, the track sweeps 90 degrees to the left. Some 75m/yds further on, turn

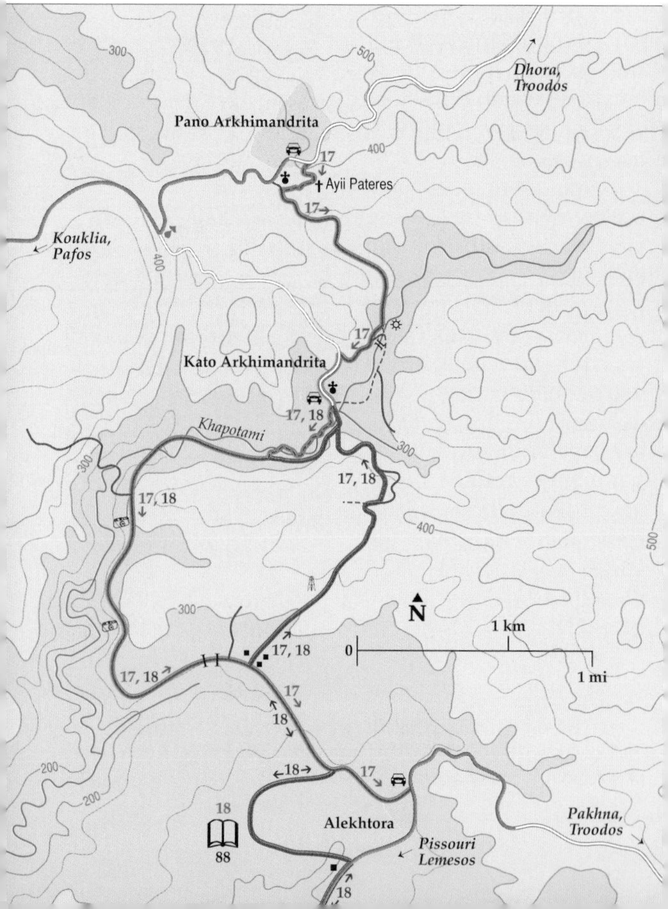

right to the brow (2h). Almost immediately after beginning the descent, take a stony path off to the left, which cuts off two bends in the track. Meet the track again and follow it down to the still-fertile and cultivated valley of Kato Arkhimandrita and your car (2h30min).

Pano Arkhimandrita is situated among vineyards perched on hillsides, and the effect of the scenery when you first arrive is quite breathtaking. There is more to come.

Clearly signed on the south side of the village is is a concrete road to 'The Cave of 318 Fathers'. Follow this and then go down some steps to the hermitage of Ayii Pateres, a tiny shrine nestling in a rock crevice. Herein is preserved a quantity of human bones. It is said they are of 318 saints who arrived on the coast at Pissouri in days of yore after fleeing persecution in Syria, only to meet an untimely death at the hands of local heathens. Your welcome in Arkhimandrita will be warmer, especially in either of the two coffee shops where locals will happily talk about their tiny community.

Visit the SHRINE (see drawing above), respecting the 'don't touch' appeal, then **begin the walk** by going under the railings about 5m/yds back from the shrine, onto a short grassy path. This leads to a 1m/3ft scramble down to a track. Follow the track to the right as it passes below the village CHURCH and meets a broader track just below the road. Turn left and continue downhill, sometimes on concrete sections, but without deviation. Just before reaching the valley floor, turn right on a track (concreted at the outset). Soon look out for a RUINED MILL, almost hidden in shrubbery on the left. Before reaching the valley floor again, fork right on another track (**31min**). (The left fork leads, in about 100m/yds, to an interesting old HUMP-BACKED BRIDGE.) Fork left at a junction on another concrete stretch and go straight ahead at the next junction.

Continue round the slopes, with the Arkhimandrita Valley deep on the left, and reach the abandoned village of **Kato Arkhimandrita** (**45min**). Walk through the village and at **49min** come to a clear path off to the right, just before the river bed (usually dry). Here you have two options — take this meandering path which criss-crosses the river bed or go past the river bed to a crossroads and take the track to the right. The path is the more enjoyable option, as it follows either bank of the river. You will see the track up to your left before you join it after the fourth river crossing, at an open area (**1h10min**).

From this point you are heading into the spectacular **Khapotami Gorge**. Towering cliffs, birds of prey wheeling overhead, an infinite variety of trees and plants, lizards scampering at your feet … the holiday beaches seem a long way from this kind of Cyprus. Follow the track, sometimes just the boulders of the river bed, as it runs all the way through the walkable part of the gorge.

At about **1h35min**, at a fork, your track widens and heads up to the left, out of the gorge. (The track to the right crosses the river and zigzags up the opposite side of the gorge.) You will get steadily more impressive views down into the impassable part of the gorge as you climb.

Eventually, the track levels out and contours round two sharp left-hand bends, the gorge always on your right. Notice a pylon in the distance and rise gently to pass through two gates, into a vineyard (**2h05min**). *(For the circular walk, ignore the first track off left, 60m past the second gate; take the next, wide track to the left, some 150m further on.)* The main walk continues ahead for somewhat over 1km into **Alekhtora** (**2h35min**).

Top: priest at Pano Arkhimandrita (left) and wall painting inside his church (middle); church in the ruined village of Kato Arkhimandrita (right). Left: Arkhimandrita's green valley

18 CIRCUIT FROM ALEKHTORA

Distance: 6km/3.7mi; 2h18min
Grade: quite easy, with a climb/descent of about 125m/400ft
Equipment: walking boots or stout shoes, sunhat, water, picnic
How to get there and return: 🚌 to Alekhtora. Park at the junction near the 'Alekhtora' sign — 1.5km south of Alekhtora, where the road makes a near-90-degree right turn, next to a fruit-packing factory (see map on page 88).
Alternative walk: Alekhtora — Lakko tou Frankou — Khapotami Gorge — Alekhtora (17km/10.6mi; 5h30min; strenuous and long, with ascents/descents of about 400m/1300ft). Equipment and access as main walk, but take *plenty of water* and note that this walk is not suitable in high summer, as there is almost no shade. Combine this walk with Walk 17 for a long day out. After completing this walk, head north along the road towards Alekhtora for 1km, then fork left on a track (by a disused fruit-packing shed on the left). Skirting round vineyards, you meet the track followed at the end of Walk 17: turn left and after about 1km turn right on a track with farm buildings and shelters on both sides (you will see a pylon to the left of this track, above you). Close to the top of the ridge, the track sweeps 90 degrees to the left. Some 75m/yds further on, turn right to the brow. Almost immediately after beginning the descent, take a stony path off to the left, which cuts off two bends in the track. Meet the track again and follow it down to the abandoned village of Kato Arkhimandrita. Now pick up Walk 17 at the 45min-point, to walk through the Kapotami Gorge and back towards Alekhtora, picking up your outward track round the vineyards and turning right at the disused fruit-packing shed, to round the vineyards and return to your car.

This is an interesting walk, mainly through farming land. The old hamlet of Lakko tou Frankou provides a fascinating insight into life past and, if you haven't already done Walk 17, the spectacular views into the gorge will surely whet your appetite for it.

Start out at the junction by the 'ALEKHTORA' sign. Follow a rough road (soon becoming a track, sometimes cobbled) through vineyards. Go straight on at a junction

Goat enclosure typical of the island's interior

(**11min**), still gently climbing. You pass another fruit-packing depot and an enclosure sheltering goats with with longest, floppiest ears your're ever likely to see! The track soon starts zigzagging up to the antenna visible above. Make use of three obvious short-cuts and reach the top at the solar-powered ANTENNA (**34min**, Picnic 18a). Have a breather, if not a picnic, and survey the countryside you have just traversed.

Then turn right and follow a track past the antenna. As you can see on the map, we're heading for an overview of the Khapotami Gorge, the setting for Walk 17. Goats graze amongst the carob trees, and large flocks of jackdaws screech noisily. At a junction where there are goat troughs on the right (**45min**) you can take either fork. The tracks soon meet and head towards a large animal FARM (goats, sheep and horses) on the hillside ahead. Reach it (**1h01min**), making for its left-hand side. Step down through old stone terraces to the KHAPOTAMI OVERLOOK (**1h08min**; Picnic 18b), for really spectacular views into the Khapotami Gorge.

When you have enjoyed a break in these beautiful surroundings, walk back up to the animal farm and, facing away from both it and the ridge, follow a track

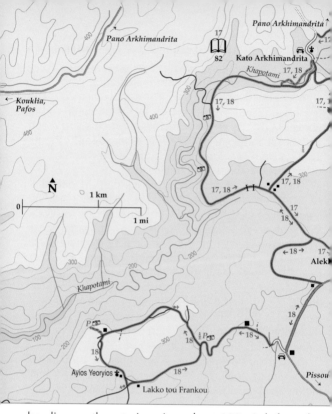

heading south, entering pines about 100m/yds from the farm. Fork left after a few minutes and notice a white triangulation point over to the left — this confirms your route. The rough track descends and you will then see a tiny church ahead. The surface improves and gets you to the church, **Ayios Yeoryios**, at **1h23min**. It has white walls, a faded blue roof and no windows.

Immediately beyond the church is the ruin of an 18th-century 'KHAN' or coaching station. Just beyond this, fork right to a junction, where a stone trough sits beside an old well, now dry. This perhaps gave rise to this area's name of **Lakko tou Frankou** (Well of the French).

Turn left here and in a few minutes pass a partially renovated farmhouse, all closed up, and cowsheds, open and obviously still very much in use. The track rises gradually, cobbled in places, indicating that this was perhaps an important trans-village link in bygone days. Reach the antenna junction of your outward route (**1h48min**) and descend, remembering the short cuts. Say 'hello' to the long-eared goats and return to your car at the 'ALEKHTORA' sign (**2h18min**).

19 FONTANA AMOROSA COASTAL PATH

See map on reverse of touring map; see also photos pages 23, 92-93

Distance: 6km/3.7mi, 1h45min

Grade: quite easy, almost level walking

Equipment: stout shoes, sunhat, water, picnic, swimming things

How to get there and return: 🚗 car or 🚐 (Timetable F1) to/from Lachi, then 🚤 from Lachi to Fontana Amorosa; 🚐 (Timetable F1) or taxi from the Baths of Aphrodite back to Lachi

A wonderful walk with amazing views around the compass. Birdsong, butterflies, tiny lizards avoiding your feet, and a backdrop of mountains. What more could one ask for? This walk takes you through unspoiled Cyprus, and long may it remain so.

The best approach to Fontana Amorosa is from the sea, so head initially to Lachi, where a boat can be hired to take you there (ask at the Lachi Water Sports Centre). Sharing the boat journey with others will ensure that the cost is very reasonable. There is no proper landing area; the boatman will ask you to leap ashore on a hot and rocky outcrop which, at first sight, hardly merits its name. In reality the 'fountain of love' is a 5-metre deep well (which you may not even find), but it doesn't matter! You have only come for the pleasure of walking back to the Baths of Aphrodite. For a longer ramble, it is interesting to walk to the very western tip of the island, Cape Arnauti (an extra 3km/2mi return), passing the wrecked freighter Agnello on the way.

The track from **Fontana Amorosa starts out** in an area of scrub. It may take a minute to locate, but once found, there is no problem. Simply head back eastwards and enjoy the environment. The route wanders through scrub on both sides, but in **10min** you should be enjoying good views of the sea. In **20min** come to a large WARNING SIGN ABOUT MILITARY EXERCISES and take good notice: don't touch anything suspicious-looking. Equally, don't be deterred by the 'red flag' aspect of this walk. It really is spectacular, with no evidence of the military, except for the signs.

At **40min** the track turns inland for no more than 50m/yds to avoid a gully, then it gains height as it continues eastwards. At about **45min** you may catch sight of a cairn on a rock to the right, and of a particularly attractive cove down left. At **1h10min** the route climbs more steeply, but not for long, and the views from this level are the finest of the walk.

89

At the end of this stretch, one gets a panoramic view over the **Baths of Aphrodite**, which should be reached in about **1h45min**. For this last descent, keep to the broader track on the right, not the narrower way through low-lying trees… lest you disturb the goats.

From the Baths you can catch a bus back to Lachi in summer, or call for a taxi when you arrive. You *could* even walk to Lachi along shingle beaches and the edges of fields, but the way is unclear, the going frustrating, and the landscape indifferent compared with what has gone before.

Left: wild garlic flourishes in stony areas.
Below: a delightfully secluded cove,
seen from above the Baths of Aphrodite;
the camping site is nicely situated on the
cliffs in the background.

20 THE 'APHRODONIS' TRAIL

See map on reverse of touring map; see also photographs opposite and on pages 17, 23 and 95 (bottom)

Distance: about 7.5km/4.7mi; 2h50min, whichever trail you choose

Grade: moderate, with a steep climb of 250m/820ft at the start. The Aphrodite trail climbs an additional 100m/330ft. Both trails involve zigzag descents on fairly loose rubble in places; *you must be sure-footed and have a head for heights.*

Equipment: stout shoes or boots, sunhat, water, picnic; optional trekking pole(s)

How to get there and return: 🚗 car or taxi to/from the Baths of Aphrodite tourist pavilion. Or 🚌 from Polis (Timetable F1; summer only)

Walkers who have trod the Fontana Amorosa coastal path (Walk 19) know how special the views are in this 'top left-hand corner' of Cyprus. Imagine how much more exciting those views are from 300 metres (1000 feet) higher up! Thanks to a pair of Forestry Department nature trails ('Aphrodite' and 'Adonis'), you can enjoy these views and at the same time learn more about the flora and fauna of the Akamas. A booklet fully explaining points of interest is available from tourist offices, or from the Forestry Department office near the Baths of Aphrodite tourist pavilion.

The two trails share a common ascent at the start, lasting a little over an hour. The Aphrodite trail then heads northwest, climbing to skirt the Moutti tis Sotiras plateau, and offers incomparable views towards Cape Arnauti. The Adonis trail heads in the opposite direction initially, giving splendid views over the coastline southeast of the Baths of Aphrodite. I take you up to the 'decision point', then describe both trails. Whichever you choose, you're likely to come back and head the opposite way another day!

You need more than sandals or trainers for either experience, for while the routes are well marked and by no means severe, they do present some challenge to wind and limb, and the surfaces can be rocky or loose, especially on their zigzag descents (some 'Landscapers' have experienced mild vertigo on the Aphrodite descent).

The walk starts at the CAR PARK close to the TOURIST PAVILION. Head west to the clearly signed start to the trails. You reach **Loutra Aphroditis** (the **Baths of Aphrodite**) at TRAIL POINT 5; Aphrodite was said to sport with lovers here. Follow the sign 'NATURE TRAIL', crossing the bed of the **Argaki tou Pyrgou** and heading up steps. At the top, turn sharp left on a narrow rocky uphill path — the highest of the paths available. The coastal track from

Fontana Amorosa (Walk 19), your return route, is lower down. Climb steeply to TRAIL POINT 8 (**15min**) and keep left at another fork two minutes later. As you rise, you'll notice a small island with a cross, which commemorates a diver who lost his life near the island some years ago. About 50m past TRAIL POINT 10 you are directed sharply up to the right, and you very soon come to TRAIL POINT 11. There are seats near here from where you can enjoy your first really good views over the coast (**35min**; Picnic 20, photograph page 17). Walk through a clearing which is level for about 200m/yds, but ahead you'll see (and feel!) the trail rising sharply. It can be a sweat, but the pain doesn't last long! At the top there's a welcome bench, from which to look back to Lachi and beyond to Polis.

Some 3-4 minutes after TRAIL POINT 20 turn left. You will come to a large wooded hollow with a GIANT OAK TREE and the substantial remains of **Pyrgos tis Rigaenas** (Queen's Shelter; **1h10min**, photograph page 95), believed to be the site of a medieval monastery. Nearby is a welcome SPRING (but it *may* be dry in summer). This is another excellent area for picnicking (Picnic 20), while you decide which of the trails to follow — **Aphrodite or Adonis**; both are signposted from the hollow (as is another nature trail, Smiyies, which is followed in Walk 21).

Aphrodite (A25 to A49): Follow the signposted track which rises in a northerly direction. After TRAIL POINT A30 leave the track on a short-cut path to the right, passing a flourish of rock roses. Following signs, zigzag up to TRAIL POINT A35, where there is a viewpoint up to the left on the plateau of **Moutti tis Sotiras** (370m/1215ft). But you will have equally stunning view towards Cape Arnauti from TRAIL POINT A37, as you zigzag down the narrowing path. *Take care* where the surface is loose. You join the coastal track from Fontana Amorosa at around **2h20min** and pass another SPRING a few minutes later. After a short climb you finish up back at the TOURIST PAVILION in about **2h50min**. This is a marvellous walk at any time of year, but in spring you may have the bonus of spotting the Cyprus tulip.

Adonis (B25 to B55): The trail climbs a short distance, past juniper trees. Near POINT B29 you briefly join a forestry road; keep left downhill. Beyond a fine stand of Calabrian pines (TRAIL POINT B30), keep left downhill on a path, leaving the track. When you come to TRAIL POINT B34 (**1h45min**), turn left (the way straight ahead also leads to the Smiyies trail and Walk 21). There's a WATER TROUGH here, of alleged drinking quality, but you may prefer your bottle. There's a really lovely descent now,

to the right of a gully, and the whole area is covered with wild flowers in springtime. Simply follow the trail numbers (there's a long gap between B46 and B47). At TRAIL POINT B50 you come to a stunning viewpoint (photograph page 23), from where you can see your zigzag descent to the **Baths of Aphrodite**, which you should reach after **2h50min** or so.

Cape Arnauti from the Aphrodite trail

21 AKAMAS GOLD

See map on reverse of touring map   **Distance**: 13km/8mi; 3h30min

Grade: moderate, with ascents of about 250m/820ft

Equipment: walking boots or stout shoes, sunhat, water, picnic, *torch*

How to get there and return: 🚗 car or taxi to/from Neokhorio (via Lachi)

Short walk for motorists: Smiyies nature trail (6.5km/4mi; 2h; easy). Drive on the rough road out of Neokhorio to the Smiyies picnic site (see map; signposted) and start and end the walk there.

Even shorter walk for motorists: Do the Short walk above, but turn off the ridge track at nature trail signpost No 9, where there is a sign 'Smiyies 2km'.

Alternative walks: Below are just two possibilities from the many walk options in this area (see map on reverse of touring map). Take a taxi to start; return from the Baths by 🚐 (Timetable F1, summer only).

1   Neokhorio — Smiyies — Aphrodite trail — Baths of Aphrodite (13km/8mi; 3h15min; an additional climb of 100m/330ft). After visiting the mine (1h30min), regain the higher track and continue along, then turn right at a military warning sign to link up with the Aphrodite trail (Walk 20). When you reach it after 500m/yds, fork left to climb round the Moutti tis Sotiras plateau and then descend to the Baths. (You could also turn *right* on the trail and descend more directly to the Baths from Pyrgos tis Rigaenas.)

2   Neokhorio — Smiyies — Adonis trail — Baths of Aphrodite (10km/6.2mi; 2h30min). From the mine, continue on the Smiyies nature trail, to join the Adonis nature trail near point No B34. Keep ahead to descend to the Baths.

Is it a gold mine? Or was it just magnesium ore that Cypriot miners extracted from the abandoned workings we find on this grand route? Let's go see, but don't give up the day job yet! The real rewards on this day's outing are the magnificent views over Kolpos Khrysokhous (Golden Bay) and the Akamas Forest in the south. I have given the distance for motorists who start and finish the walk at Neokhorio, but if you're up to it, I urge you to consider one of the longer Alternative walks.

Start out at the CHURCH in **Neokhorio**. Walk west along the road to some WATER TANKS on the edge of the village, where the road reverts to track and forks (**10min**). Head right here, towards Ayios Minas. The left fork would take you to the goats of Androlikou (see page 24)… another day, perhaps? Beyond the restored church of **Ayios Minas** (**40min**) you come to the popular **Smiyies** PICNIC SITE (**50min**; Picnic 21). Keep to the left of it, passing the start of a signposted circuit round the **Pissouromouti** peak. (This optional detour, including a climb to the top, would give you a magnificent view over the whole coast: allow 3km/2mi and an extra 125m/400ft of ascent; 1h.)

Come at **55min** to a T-junction of tracks on a ridge

Some say this abandoned mine once produced gold... but old maps indicate magnesium. Whatever the end product, this is the old smelter. The galleried workings of the mine can be explored with care; take a torch, and don't go alone. Below: Pyrgos tis Rigaenas (Alternative walk and Walk 20)

('Route A' in the 4WD Options for Car tour 1 on page 24). Turn right and start enjoying the views, firstly to the left, and later, in both directions. There'll likely be a welcome breeze, even on a hot day.

You'll shortly see the turn-off to a FIRE-WATCH STATION, then a sign-post back to 'Smiyies 2km — Short Way' on your right *(the 'Even shorter walk')*. Keep ahead and look out, off to the right, for a level track skirting round the hillside. Ignore it but, 150m/yds further on, watch for a second track (signposted as a NATURE TRAIL): it drops down sharply to the right. This leads to the ABANDONED MINE WORKINGS (**1h30min**). On the left is the smelting furnace (what's left of it) and, to the right, entrances to the old mine's galleries. *If you have a torch*, it's possible to explore some of them for a short distance, but take care (there are deep pits inside these mines!), and don't venture in there alone. No gold nuggets? I'm sorry!

You now have several options.

For the main walk, follow the track that drops down to the left of the smelting furnace, then fork right near TRAIL POINT 14 (turpentine tree) on the **Smiyies nature trail**. This will bring you back to the PICNIC SITE at **2h40min** or so, and to **Neokhorio** at around **3h30min**.

For Alternative walk 1, return to the upper track and proceed as described above to reach the **Aphrodite trail** at Pyrgos tis Rigaenas; then see notes on page 93.

For Alternative walk 2 continue as the main walk, but fork *left* on the Smiyies trail, to reach the **Adonis trail** near a SPRING and SIGNPOST B34; then see notes on page 93.

A great day's walking, whatever your choice of routes.

22 KRITOU TERRA AND TERRA

Distance: 4km/2.5mi, 1h30min

Grade: easy descent and reascent of about 150m/500ft

Equipment: stout shoes, sunhat, water, picnic

How to get there and return: 🚌 to/from Kritou Terra (a detour on Car tour 1, page 23). Park near the taverna.

Alternative walk: Drousseia circuit (3.5km/2.2mi; 50min; easy, with an ascent/descent of just 40m/130ft). This short but appealing circuit makes an ideal leg-stretcher. Park behind the Droushia Heights Hotel. Walk up into the village, passing Finikas Tavera. Turn right between two coffee houses and go down to the open-air theatre. Go straight ahead on Odos Karis (signed in Greek) and turn left on a track at a green arrow (10min). You get fantastic views of the Troodos Mountains and the north coast and pass an interesting rock outcrop (20min; Picnic 22). Proceed through vineyards, to another track (28min). Your way is to the left, but first take a short detour to the tiny modern church along to the right; then return and, soon on tarmac, regain Drousseia (50min).

This is a lovely, short and very interesting stroll — easy to get to from Pafos, via Kathikas, or from the Lachi-Polis area via the E709. It starts in the village of Kritou Terra from the restored village springs near the taverna.

Start out by walking from the TAVERNA into **Kritou Terra** (*don't* go along the Terra road). You pass a turning right which leads to the church shown opposite (just before a coffee shop on the right with an external iron staircase). On the left is the old village FLOUR MILL, with a vine on its terraced roof. Beyond here is a low wall, over which you will see a series of holes in the rock beside a water channel. This was formerly the communal laundry.

The way drops a little, and you'll pass a small chapel on a rocky outcrop off to the right. Some 100m/yds further on, there is a metal grating in the road: turn left just beyond it, on an indistinct path (near a wooden gate). The path may be overgrown in places, and you should watch out for stones underfoot, especially after rain.

After crossing a streambed, the path widens out, and you now have an easy walk to **Terra** (**45min**) — among a myriad of wild flowers in springtime. Terra has a semi-

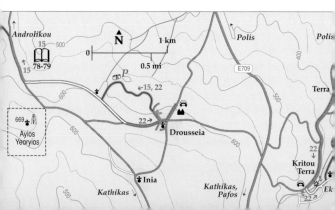

Top: the Byzantine church of Ayia Ekaterina lies not far from Drousseia and the Terras. Since this medieval ruin is more complete than many on Cyprus and contains some faded wall paintings, it is well worth a short (5km) detour during Car tour 1. To reach it, take the crudely signposted road from Kritou Terra (see map — not the Terra road). The church can also be reached within 2km from the Paphos–Polis road at a marked turn-off 1km south of Skoulli. Above and left: around Terra

derelict look… indeed many of its houses are unoccupied, but there has been a settlement here since Roman times. Nowadays some of the Turkish-owned houses abandoned during the 1974 occupation of the north are being restored by Greek tenants through a government conservation scheme.

Coming through Terra village, you will see the old MOSQUE with cypress trees 'guarding' it. Linger a while in Terra, and maybe talk with a resident or two. It's a lovely peaceful place. Then bear left near the mosque and follow the road back to **Kritou Terra (1h30min)**. Visit the taverna near the entrance before you leave, and help keep a traditional Cypriot community thriving!

23 MILIOU • THELETRA • MILIOU

Distance: 10.5km/6.5mi; 2h55min

Grade: strenuous, with several steep ascents and descents (300m/1000ft overall). All tracks are good, although there could be a couple of muddy sections after rain.

Equipment: walking boots or stout shoes, sunhat, picnic, water; trekking poles useful

How to get there and return: 🚌 to/from Miliou, a detour from the 86km-point on Car tour 1. Shortly before reaching Miliou, pass the Agii Anargyri Hotel, then park in a small lay-by just after crossing a bridge with iron railings.

Short walk: Miliou views (2.5km/1.6mi; 45min; easy, with an ascent/descent of only 60m/200ft). Follow the main walk to the 25min-point, enjoy the splendid views, and return the same way.

This is a glorious hike with far-reaching views, sometimes over the whole walk route. The deserted village of Kato Theletra is fascinating to explore and provides a welcome shady pause before the second leg of the walk. Be sure to follow the instructions carefully — the whole area is cultivated and covered with a myriad of tracks.

Start the walk at the LAY-BY in **Miliou**: head back the way you came, climb up past the AGII ANARGYRI HOTEL, and notice the high ridge overlooking the valley to the right. The return route runs along the ridge, a little below the top. Look out also for resident peregrine falcons, easily identified by their alternate flapping and gliding.

As the road bends sharp left go straight ahead on a concrete track (**8min**). At a fork, old Kato Theletra is visible in the distance, with the church of new Pano Theletra perched above it — and the whole walk is laid out before you. Go right and descend (now on a dirt track) into the **Neradhes Valley**. Cross the watercourse ('Stream of the Fairies'; **14min**), then bear right and start climbing, ignoring tracks off left and right. Just after a steep sandy section, ignore another track left and one right (**21min**). Continue up to a junction of tracks (**25min**). To the left are panoramic views across groves to the hills beyond, with the village of Yiolou just visible on the ridge (Picnic 23). *(The Short walk turns back here.)*

Go straight ahead on the middle track and within about 250m/yds, at a fork, go uphill to the right (**29min**). There is a faded blue arrow on the wall here, and more old blue waymarking will occasionally confirm your route to Theletra. After a further 250m fork up right again, and soon start to descend towards the Neradhes Gorge.

Go left at the next junction (**36min**), then left again, downhill, at a fork, between almond groves and vineyards. Cross a narrow ravine (**44min**) and, at the next

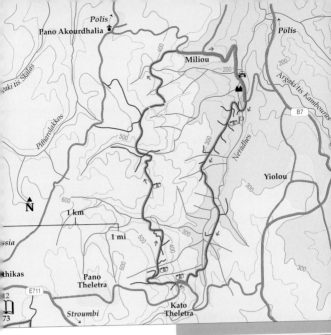

fork, go left downhill. Follow the main track as it crosses the fertile **Neradhes** streambed, lined with giant reeds (**48min**). Go straight on at a junction, following the streambed. This damp area, where there is sometimes a sizeable pool, attracts birds; tread quietly so as not to disturb them. At a fork, go uphill to the left and undulate gently alongside the stream for a short time, eventually crossing it again. The track (sometimes concreted) then zigzags steeply uphill. Pause often to admire the surroundings and catch your breath.

The track levels out a bit and you reach the road which passes through **Kato Theletra** (**1h09min**). The ongoing walk turns up sharp right here, but you will surely wish to explore. The houses are now deserted, but there

Kato Theletra

are often locals around, tending the vines and other fruit trees. You can learn more about the history of this fascinating village in the excellent booklet, 'Discover Laona', available at the Visitor Centre in Kathikas (Walk 12).

As you continue the walk on a wide road, marvel at the extent of the Troodos Mountains across the valley. Where the road bends sharp left (**1h18min**), leave it on a concrete downhill track straight ahead (by a hunting sign and a painted red circle). The track soon reverts to dirt and follows the gorge, passing a smallholding with noisy loose dogs. Ignore all tracks off left and right to groves and the like, but at a major junction (**1h25min**), execute a U-turn to the right, to round the head of the gorge and climb a concrete section. Go right at a fork, just opposite a smallholding.

Follow the main track, sometimes concreted, past a track going down right to a rocky outcrop. As you now contour around the slopes you'll see the village of Yiolou over to the right, backed by Mount Olympus. On reaching a SMALL OPEN AREA (**1h39min**) ignore the track going back sharp right, then fork left. Ignore minor tracks and follow the main track to another fork. Keep right. Contour round fertile terracing, past a stone hut and vineyards (with a less than fastidious owner).

As a track comes in from the left continue downhill on a rather rough, stony track — take care here (**1h 49min**). Cross a dip and rise steeply to a multiple junction (**2h05min**). Ignore the track off 90° left; take the next track, going half-left, downhill (relief!), and notice Miliou below to the right. Shortly after another stone hut, your track is lined both sides by electricity poles. Keep right at a junction. At the first sharp left-hand bend, the concrete ceases for a while; it starts again as the track becomes a road and continues descending, following the line of cables.

Where the road goes under the CABLES (**2h20min**) take a short-cut on an eroded, overgrown track down to the left. Back at the road, fork left immediately and continue, always winding downwards, round the gorge. Join the road coming in from Kathikas on the left and reach the first houses in **Miliou** (**2h36min**). You pass the village coffee house off to your left. If you stop here for a quick beer, it turns into a meal as you're served lots of little dishes of snacks (*meze*) in a typical gesture of Cypriot hospitality. Continue straight on, winding downhill and out of the village, back to the LAY-BY (**2h55min**).

24 ALAMANOU TO GOVERNOR'S BEACH

Distance: 5-8km/3-5mi; 1h30min-2h10min

Grade: very easy, but sometimes rough underfoot; no shade

Equipment: stout shoes, sunhat, water, swimwear

How to get there: 🚗 car to Ayios Yeoryios Alamanou or to a large parking area by the shore, south of the monastery. Or 🚌 (Timetables B6, C5) to the Ayios Yeoryios Alamanou turn-off on the old road between Lemesos and Larnaka.

To return: 🚌 from the old main road above Governor's Beach (Timetables B6, C5) — back to the Ayios Yeoryios Alamanou turn-off, from where you can walk to your car, or back to base. Or taxi back to your car. There is also a 🚌 which runs from Governor's Beach to the waterfront hotels in Lemesos between May and September: check up-to-date times with a tourist office.

Note: If travelling by bus, reconfirm with a tourist office or the operator that the buses you plan to use are travelling on the old road and will stop at the monastery turn-off and the beach.

If Governor's Beach were white or golden in colour, developers would have had their way with it by now. But its grey (though clean) appearance has saved this popular retreat from touristic blandness. No one would include it in a list of the world's great watering-holes, but its informal — even ramshackle — atmosphere makes for a happy finish to this easiest of strolls. The walk can be accomplished with ease in either direction, but hire-car drivers might find it most agreeable to start at the

The blue and white galleries and courtyard at the monastery of Ayios Yeoryios Alamanou: the sisters here sell flowers, jam, eggs and chickens, and a lone monk occupies a single room near the entrance, wherein he eats, sleeps, and paints icons which the visitor can buy.

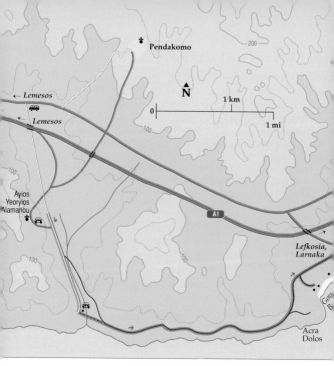

monastery of Ayios Yeoryios Alamanou, walk to Governor's Beach for a swim and lunch, then return. The monastery is not particularly ancient, but its blue and white galleries and courtyard are very pretty, as you can see in the photograph on page 101.

To **start the walk** at **Ayios Yeoryios Alamanou**, take the dirt road off to the right just back from the monastery car park. (Since this road can be heavily trafficked at times and raise a lot of dust, you may prefer to drive down to the car park by the coast to begin.) On foot, you reach the sea and a shingle beach in about **30min**; there is a good fish taverna here, but it may be seasonal. Turn left along the beach for a few minutes, then climb briefly onto a track which winds along to Governor's Beach, hugging the waterline.

At the headland of **Cape Dolos** you will look down over the **Governor's Beach** area, and the best approach from here is to head inland a little, to pick up the sign-posted track down to the tavernas, of which there are several to choose from. Your journey from the monastery should take about **1h45min**.

From here walk on to the junction with the old coastal road, where you can flag down a bus in either direction. Or take a taxi back to your car if the effort of lunch has been too much!

25 KELLAKI TO YERMASOYIA

Distance: 15km/9.3mi; 5h

Grade: moderate to strenuous because of the length; you should be sure-footed and have a head for heights. Ascent 240m/790ft; descent 550m/1800ft

Equipment: stout shoes or boots, sunhat, water, picnic

How to get there: 🚕 taxi to Kellaki; ask the driver to drop you about 1.6km south of the village, at a junction where Prastio and the Kyparissia trail are clearly signposted.
To return: 🚌 from Yermasoyia to Lemesos (Timetable B10)

Short walk: Phinikaria fisherman's trail (1.5km/0.9mi; 30min or more; easy — trainers will suffice). Drive across the wall of Yermasoyia Dam and on to the signposted nature trail car park just past Phinikaria. Walk down from the car park and under the archway, where there is an information board and map. It will take about 30 minutes to walk the circuit around the peninsula, but it is also worth climbing the steps to the hexagonal shelter on the central hill (Picnic 25a).

Alternative circuits for motorists

1 Circuit below Kyparissia (8.5km/5.3mi; 2h40min; moderate, with an ascent/descent of 200m/650ft; you should be sure-footed and have a head for heights). 🚗 Drive to the junction at the start of the main walk and drive along the forest road, following instructions for the main walk for about 1.7km, to the 31min-point. Park here, courteously, and continue following the main walk to the 1h41min-point (the path marked by a cairn; 1h10min). Turn sharp right uphill and climb through thinning pines. Wind round the slopes, rising gradually with ever-changing views. Pass a bench just after a sharp right turn and almost immediately come to a junction. Turn sharp right here; a rocky track takes you steeply up to a fork. Go right and reach a secondary peak of Kyparissia, where there is a hexagonal wooden shelter (1h38min, Picnic 25b). Views in all directions give you a matchless panorama — from Mount Olympus in the north to the dam in the south, Kouklia in the west and the mountains above Larnaka in the east. Continue downhill on this track, keeping left at a fork. Pass another bench, then walk under the main peak of Kyparissia to complete the loop at the 4-way junction (1h55min). Take the wide track which goes almost straight ahead and retrace your steps to your car (2h40min).

Kellaki, with the radar 'golf balls' of Mount Olympus in the distance

2 Circuit from Yermasoyia Dam (9.5km/5.9mi; 3h; quite strenuous, with an ascent/descent of 590m/1935ft). You should be sure-footed and have a head for heights. Although most of this walk is out and back, it is a brilliant hike, much of it on mountain paths — a proper hiker's day out. Drive to the start of the Short walk and park in the car park. Walk up the asphalt road and turn off left on Kyparissouvouno Street at a hunting sign (12min). This is the 2h48min-point of the main walk; referring to the map, follow the main walk in reverse back to its 1h41min-point (the path off left below Kyparissia, marked by a cairn) and then pick up the notes for *Alternative* walk 1. When you reach the 4-way junction, pick up the main walk again at the 1h18min-point and follow it back to your car (3h).

This is a long walk, but after the first hour or so it is all downhill. You'll pass from rugged mountainside to gentle countryside enjoying the varied scenery — a deep gorge, a vast dam and views to drool over.

Start the walk on the E109 road 1.6km south of Kellaki. Follow the TRAIL SIGN (similar signs will direct you to the official start of the Kyparissia nature trail in somewhat more than the 3km indicated). The tarmac ends immediately and a forest road winds down through pines

to a junction (**13min**). Go left here and then straight on at a fork (**21min**). You soon pass a little house on the left and reach a junction where you fork uphill to the right (**31min**; *Alternative walk 1 drives to this point and joins the main walk.*) You are now climbing on a steep rough track with sheer drops down left into the valley. Pause to take in the magnificent views.

Reach a junction with signs and a bench, the official start of the **Kyparissia trail** (**56min**). Go straight on past the information board canopy and follow the track sharp left uphill. You'll almost feel you are climbing to the stars! But the way soon levels out (**1h11min**) and brings you to a 4-WAY JUNCTION, also with a bench (**1h18min**). Follow the arrow pointing downhill, almost straight ahead. You pass a track joining from the right as your track becomes a path and descends more steadily. Notice the first of the very few tree identification signs on the left and then look up to the right to see the hexagonal shelter visited on Alternative walk 1 (**1h29min**; Picnic 25b). After a few short zigzags walk alongside a stream bed, then cross it (**1h36min**). Continue alongside the stream and after a short rise notice a narrow path going back up to the right, indicated by a CAIRN (**1h41min**). *(Alternative walk 1 takes this path.)*

Continue ahead. The path begins to descend more sharply and becomes more rocky. You'll soon catch your first views of the **Kyparissia Gorge** (the northerly arm of the Yermasoyia River) to the right. Wind down through pines and pause to look down to the dam and all the way past Lemesos to the Akrotiri Peninsula (**1h52min**). The path continues to descend and switches to the left side of the ridge for a while, but then back to the right as it descends to meet a track (**2h11min**). Turn left, downhill. (A short distance to the right is a large partridge pen — probably where birds are held before being released for a shoot!). This is probably the bottom end of the nature trail, but there are no signs to tell you so.

Get closer views of the dam and reservoir and in a few minutes pass a track coming in from the left. You will then find yourself heading east, away from the dam, as you begin a long zigzag. But don't worry, you'll soon change direction again as you follow this wide track, without deviation and ignoring another track uphill to

the left on a hairpin bend (**2h30min**). There's a short deviation as you reach cultivation, due to a small landslide (**2h40min**) and then another very rough track joins you from the right. This was actually a short cut from higher up, but, because it is a tricky descent, it was best not to suggest it!

You now pass fruit groves and a magnificent patch of prickly pears, then reach an asphalt road (**2h48min**). Turn right and continue to descend towards the dam. There are a few houses by the side of this road, each with superb views. As you round a left hand bend, with a dirt road joining from the right, notice a NATURE TRAIL CAR PARK opposite (**3h**, Picnic 25a). This is the starting point for the Short walk.

Continue left around the bend. After a U-bend (**3h10min**), you might be tempted by a sign to a café in **Phinikaria** up to the left — where the beer and the views are thoroughly recommended. If so, it is only a slight deviation and you can rejoin the road at the end of the village. Otherwise, meet the village road and turn right. Continue downwards on this quiet asphalt road, admiring the impressive circle of crags on the left and making use of occasional benches overlooking the **Yermasoyia Dam** on the right. Cross the DAM WALL and turn left (**4h13min**).

After about 200m turn off left on a gravel track (the

old road) which goes down to the river. It runs alongside the river, through a fertile valley and eventually becomes asphalt (**4h40min**). Around 500m/yds further on, take an asphalt road up to the right and join the main road. Turn left and reach **Yermasoyia** after a long but satisfying day's walk (**5h**). Buses to Lemesos leave quite frequently from opposite the café in the main square (by the parking meters).

View down over Yermasoyia Dam and Phinikaria from the 2h15min-point in the walk

26 MOUNT MAKHERAS

Distance: 5km/3mi; 1h30min

Grade: moderate, with an ascent/descent of under 200m/ 650ft overall

Equipment: stout shoes, sunhat, water, picnic

How to get there and return: 🚙 (4WD) to the Kionia picnic site, only accessible via jeep tracks (from Lemesos via Kellaki and Ayii Vavatsinias; from Larnaka via Kalokhorio, Sha and Mathiati; from Lefkosia via Analiondas). *NB:* If you are just visiting Makheras Monastery, there is one asphalted route at time of writing — via Odou, Pharmakas, Ghourri and Lazania — a beautiful drive (photograph pages 20-21). But beyond the monastery, the track to Kionia is too rough for normal hire cars.

Tip: The **Kionia nature trail** to Profitis Ilias Monastery is signposted on the other side of the road. The 7km-long trail runs mostly downhill to the monastery (shown on the touring map), with a climb of some 350m/1150ft on the return (14km/87mi return; 5h). The first kilometre of the path is shown on the map and highlighted in yellow.

T his journey to the Makheras Forest in the centre of Cyprus affords a stunning view in all directions after a short uphill walk and an energetic scramble along an easy ridge.

As one approaches Mount Makheras, from whatever direction, one becomes increasingly aware of the radar weather station on its summit, perched like a huge golf ball on a giant tee.

Below the peak, which is a few kilometres south of Makheras Monastery, we **begin the walk** at the **Kionia** PICNIC SITE, with tables, benches, and barbecue facilities. From the site take steps and then a track up to the main

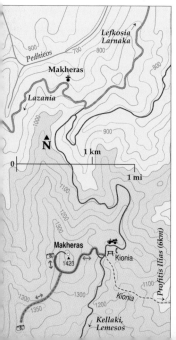

rough road to the summit and follow it uphill. There is no reason why you should not go all the way to the top for the magnificent panorama seen from just outside the gates to the radar station.

But the main walk continues from a point on the left of the road, less than 200m/yds below the gates (near a gnarled tree), where you climb over the road barrier and scramble briefly down the bank, to head for the obvious ridge. Viewed from the tree, the scramble looks easier than it is, but it is not difficult for fit walkers.

After perhaps **30min** come to a CAIRN and, 500m/yds beyond that, another CAIRN (**45min**) — a point where one feels as if the whole of Cyprus is spread below in every direction. A beautiful high place.

Retrace your steps to the **Kionia** PICNIC SITE (**1h30min**), and perhaps call at Makheras Monastery, where there is a seasonal café.

Makheras Monastery, second in importance only to Kykko, was founded in 1148, but burned down in 1530 and again in 1892. Most of what the visitor sees today dates from 1900, but the monastery is a very peaceful and beautiful retreat, especially when the almond trees blossom in February. Views from its terraces are quite impressive. In the 1950s, the EOKA organisation had a hide-out in a nearby cave, where second-in-command Gregoris Afxentiou died after a skirmish with British troops. The monastery, like Kykko, has a wealth of icons — including the one said to have inspired its founding.

27 STAVROVOUNI MONASTERY

See also photograph page 37   **Distance**: 4km/2.5mi; 2h

Grade: moderate but steep ascent/descent of 300m/1000ft on a sometimes-overgrown path; avoid in wet weather. *No shade*

Equipment: stout shoes, sunhat, water, picnic, long trousers; optional trekking pole(s)

How to get there and return: 🚗 car or taxi to Stavrovouni (a reasonable taxi excursion from Larnaka, if sharing). Park/alight at the 'Spithoudia' signpost (see below, paragraph 3). Or Lemesos–Lefkosia 🚌 (Timetable A5) to/from the Stavrovouni turn-off (add 5km/3mi overall).

Special note: Men must wear long trousers to enter Stavrovouni or Ayia Varvara, and women are not allowed inside either monastery, nor is photography permitted, but the views from the car park are still superb.

For no other reason than to experience the sheer magnificence of the views from the top (see photograph on page 37), the ascent to Stavrovouni, whether on foot or the easy way, is a must for anyone visiting Cyprus. A grand sweep of the eyes round all points of the compass takes in distant mountains, a whole spectrum of landscape colours and dozens of villages and vineyards.

On three sides, Stavrovouni ('Mountain of the Holy Cross') is almost sheer, but the fourth side is negotiable by the sturdy of foot. Approach is via the old Lefkosia–Lemesos road, or a turn-off from the new A1 road. The last few miles are hardly a delight, distinguished by a stone-crushing plant and the high-profile presence of an army camp. 'No photography' signs abound. But once this is all behind you, the magic begins.

By car, taxi or on foot, head first for the smaller monastery of **Ayia Varvara** (bee-keeping and icon-painting) and a point several hundred metres beyond, where an easily-overlooked sign indicates 'Spithoudia' to the right. Opposite here, to the left, is the **starting point**

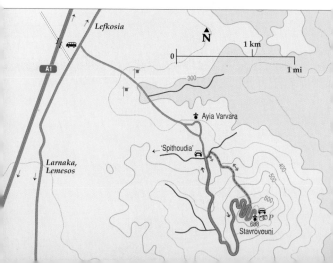

Stavrovouni Monastery: entrance and icons

of the walk. Follow this track for about 100m/yds, to pass a small PUMPING STATION. Some 25m/yds beyond the pumping station look out for the start of a narrow path on your right, rising sharply from the track.

All you have to do now is climb steadily to heaven! The way is steep and rough and not always distinct, but a useful guide is to keep a NARROW PIPE which runs to the top in view. Progress is helped by an occasional levelling-off of the path. Some two-thirds of the way up, the path leads on to the motor road, leaving one little option but to follow this a short way, as it zigzags in its final approach to the summit (688m/2250ft). Depending on your scrambling ability, you should reach **Stavrovouni Monastery** in about **45min**.

Your reward, at the top, is the finest panorama on Cyprus (Picnic 27). The monastery itself is worth looking at, but it should be noted that women visitors are not allowed inside. Stavrovouni is regarded as the oldest monastery on Cyprus, founded by St Helena circa 330, and among its artefacts is a piece of 'the true cross', now encased in silver. The monks are not unwelcoming to (male) visitors, but they are a strict, ascetic group, more interested in devotions than in running a tourist pavilion. Fruit is sometimes available from a stall near the gate, and there are toilet facilities.

The way back down is a choice of either retracing one's footsteps or walking down the motor road. You should be back at the 'SPITHOUDIA' sign at around **2h**, but more if you linger at the top ... and who would not?

28 AROUND CAPE KITI

Distance: 11km/6.8mi; 3h

Grade: easy, level walking, mostly on tracks, with some stretches along the pebbly beach. *No shade*

Equipment: stout shoes, sunhat, water, picnic, bathing things

How to get there and return: 🚗 to Kiti (Car tour 6). On entering Kiti from the Larnaka direction do not turn right towards the famous Panayia Angeloktistos church. Instead continue into the village centre and look for the other, tiny, church in the village square. Park in the car park directly opposite. Or 🚐 to/from Kiti (Timetable C9).

Shorter circuit: Lighthouse — Ayios Leonidos — Perivolia — Kiti Tower — lighthouse (8km/5mi; 2h15min; easy). Access by 🚗 to Kiti lighthouse ('Faros'). Follow the main walk from the 1h26min-point to the 2h28min-point. Go straight on, eventually heading south towards the lighthouse. Soon look out for a left turn to Larnaka (the sign is on your left). Take this road; you'll see the watchtower ahead. The road soon becomes dirt and passes between fields. Join the main walk at the 35min-point, as it comes in from the left, and follow it back to the lighthouse (2h15min). There is also a 🚐 to Perivolia (Timetable C10).

Panayia Angeloktistos ('built by angels') is a must for visitors to the Larnaka area. So before setting off, be sure to admire the beautiful mosaic of the Virgin Mary in the apse. This walk is for those who enjoy taking in the ambience of Cyprus through a gentle stroll. In truth it is a long stroll, but is basically flat. Features are a Venetian watchtower, a lighthouse and a charismatic church with an interesting cemetery. In addition you will see many tourists, expatriates and Cypriots, at leisure, and you may surprise some of them on the beach in less than formal attire!

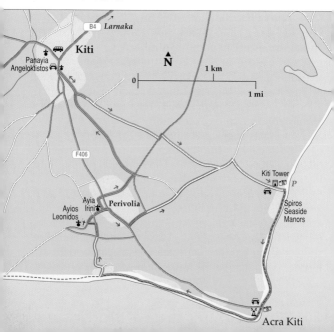

*Top: the beautifully-kept church
and cemetery of Ayios Leonidos
outside Perivolia.
Right: Kiti Tower, dating from the
15th century, is fenced off —
making photography diffcult.*

Start the walk at the tiny CHURCH in **Kiti**. Ignore the
road signed to the lighthouse and Perivolia, and take the
road straight ahead, which passes between two BANKS
and a private CLINIC. After about 500m turn right towards
'PERIVOLIA'; then, almost immediately, turn left. This road
is wide but becomes unsurfaced; the watchtower, which
is your first objective, is visible directly ahead above the
trees. With cultivated fields all around, cross an asphalt
road heading slightly to the left (**25min**). Cross a track
and reach a T-junction (**35 min**). *(The Short walk comes
in from the right here.)* Turn left and take the next right.
You will soon reach a left turn taking you up to the
Venetian watchtower, **Kiti Tower** (**48min**).

Admire the tower and the views towards Larnaka Bay,
and then continue on the dirt road to an asphalt road.
Cross this and enter a large holiday complex (SPIROS
SEASIDE MANORS). Walk between the rows of villas directly
ahead, going slightly left on a path through a wall, to
reach the BEACH (**56min**). Turn right and choose to walk
either on the beach or the 'promenade' (just an unmade
road), with fields on the right. On approaching another
resort you will have to use the beach, now sandy but
compact, until you reach the LIGHTHOUSE (**1h26min**).

Continue round the headland using the track, the
pebbly beach or the open ground — as the fancy takes

you. As the shoreline becomes more built up you have no choice but the pebbly beach for quite some time. Eventually you'll reach a large house with a DOVECOTE and lots of huge earthenware pots in its garden (**2h**). Just beyond this, leave the beach and head inland.

Take a track going left around an open field, between some villas and bearing right to an asphalt road (**2h 13min**). You have been able to see a church for some time, and you are now heading straight for it — perhaps guided by bee-eaters and a red kite. Cross this asphalt road and take another tarred road towards the church, eventually turning left on a track. **Ayios Leonidos** (**2h 19min**) and its cemetery are beautifully maintained — a tranquil resting place.

When you have wandered around and enjoyed this setting, continue on the road past the CEMETERY, sign-posted to LARNAKA. Keep straight on, passing **Ayia Irini** on the left, and turn left into 'taverna street' in **Perivolia** (**2h28min**). *(The Short walk ignores the delights of the tavernas and continues ahead here.)* Turn right at the end of this semi-pedestrianised street devoted to the pleasures of the table, pass a SUPERMARKET, and continue straight on to a crossroads, just after a sign pointing the way to the beach (**2h38min**). Turn left and follow the asphalt road past houses, then open fields, to meet your outward route and return to the tiny CHURCH in **Kiti** (**3h**).

Panayia Angeloktistos

29 AYIA NAPA • CAPE GRECO • PROTARAS

See also photograph page 40 **Distance**: 14km/8.7mi; 4h

Grade: quite easy, but with tricky stretches over razor-sharp rocks

Equipment: boots (ankle protection is *essential* in the latter part of the walk), sunhat, water, picnic, swimming things

How to get there: 🚌 to Ayia Napa (Timetable C7). Local buses also serve the Ayia Napa/Protaras/Paralimni area (Timetable D3; re-check times at a tourist office)
To return: 🚌 local Ayia Napa/Protaras/Paralimni (Timetable D3)

Short walk: This walk can be shortened at almost any point by reaching the coast road and flagging down a bus, or calling for a taxi from any of the hotels. Stout shoes will suffice as far as Kermia Beach.

The far reaches of any island always hold fascination for the traveller, and this southeastern corner of Cyprus is no exception. It is easily accessible too — Ayia Napa is one of the island's most popular tourist centres. This walk takes in sandy beaches, quiet coves, a radar-topped headland and an attractively-sited church.

Begin the walk in **Ayia Napa**, just north of the GRECIAN SANDS HOTEL (south of the MARINA HOTEL), where the road swings round to the left. Follow the palm-planted seaside promenade eastwards (Picnic 29), experiencing little sandy beaches, rocky inlets and, at about **40min**, **Kermia Beach** and its apartments.

A few minutes beyond here, the promenade ends and the going gets tricky if you want to keep to the coast, rather than follow the cairned inland path. Underfoot the rocks are sharp-edged. It is not difficult to pick a way through them, but great care should be taken to avoid ankle injury. Progress here will be slower, but you will have a fine view of inlets where waves crash into sea caves (see overleaf).

At around **1h15min**, perhaps sooner, you will approach the dominant HEADLAND which has been in view throughout the walk (but it's not Cape Greco!). Better here to move away from the sea, and join the track which skirts its base. A worthwhile detour is to enjoy one of the Forestry Department nature trails on this headland (highlighted in yellow on our map), with splendid views over Cape Greco and along to Ayia Napa. From the top of this flat headland (93m) one can even pick out Stavro-vouni (Walk 27) in the west and — on very clear days — see the mountains on the far side of the Med. It's just 1km by track from the top to the main road, where you could catch a bus and end the walk.

If you are pressing on to Cape Greco, keep to (or rejoin) the track at the base of the headland, round it, then catch a first glimpse of the cape with its lighthouse and the relay masts of Radio Monte Carlo. A little further on, look to a military radar installation high on the left. Keep well to the right of a cultivated area and climb a low hill, beyond which is a path leading down to the **Cape Greco** road. You can turn right here to get closer to the radio masts, but a locked gate prevents access to the cape itself.

It is easier to make for the eastern side of the cape and head for the picturesque little church of **Ayii Anargyri** (**2h**). From here, head up the rough road that leads to the

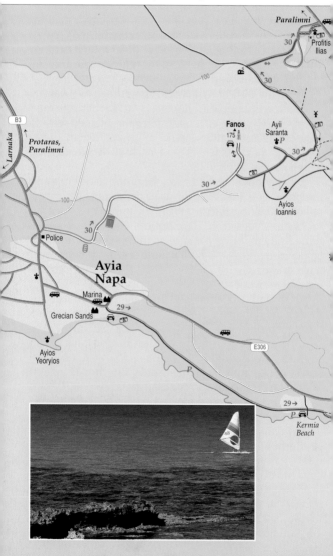

main road and end the walk by catching a bus back to Ayia Napa here if you wish. Otherwise, look for a track off to the right, leading along the edge of a not-very-high cliff, to sandy **Konnos Bay** (visible from Ayii Anargyri). At about **2h15min** come to a road zigzagging down to the bay, but before reaching the beach cross a BRIDGE on the left (signposted) and follow a track overlooking the beach.

This track soon peters out on a rock-strewn hillside. But 'Landscapers' do not worry about small problems like this! They keep going, guide in hand, clambering

Looking back to Ayia Napa from the sea caves east of Kermia Beach

over rocks, following the vaguest of paths which at first dips towards the sea (just beyond the sand) and then climbs the hillside again, to a levelling-off point from which there are pleasing views back over Konnos Bay towards Cape Greco. Some miles off the cape there is believed to lie the wreck of a 15th-century Genoese ship, as yet undiscovered.

Walk through an area of rock falls and dead trees with another, more rocky bay down to the right, and come shortly to a distinct track. Bear left for a moment to observe **Cyclop's Cave** in the hillside, but return to follow the edge of a cliff, skirting a cultivated area (**2h45min**). Vertigo is a small risk, but easily avoided. Within a minute or two, you may feel that the way ahead is at first sight impossible.

Nonsense! It is just an old QUARRY that represents a modest challenge to the nimble-footed. The way through is far from distinct, so pick your own best route through this miniature 'lost world' of boulders and undergrowth, emerging at a level area on the far side. A broad track bears left, but keep seawards for a minute or two, then turn left to walk parallel with the shore, about 100m/yds inland. To the left are a few houses, ahead is a WINDMILL, and away to the right a jagged, rocky area leading to the sea. Explore it if you wish, but watch your ankles!

From here, progress is over a completely flat coastal strip. You will walk through farmland, over rocks, and round sandy inlets — a relatively unspoiled corner of Cyprus (save for a few hotels) which has a lot of charm. You should reach **Protaras** after about **4h**.

30 AYIA NAPA TO PROFITIS ILIAS

See map pages 116-117; see also photographs on pages 40, 116, 117

Distance: 8km/5mi; 2h   **Grade**: quite easy; little climbing

Equipment: walking boots or stout shoes, sunhat, water, picnic

How to get there: 🚌 to Ayia Napa (Timetable C7). Local buses also serve the Ayia Napa/Protaras/Paralimni area (Timetable D3; re-check times at a tourist office)

To return: 🚌 local Ayia Napa/Protaras/Paralimni (Timetable D3)

Short walk: Ayii Saranta (2km/1.2mi; 45min return). 🚗 drive the first part of the walk, along the rough road, and park short of the transmitter tower. Then use the notes below from the 35min- to the 50min-point and return the same way.

Tip: The CTO has also signposted a trail running *inland* between Konnos Bay and Profitis Ilias via Ayios Ioannis and Ayii Saranta. This route is highlighted in yellow on our map; we pick up their route just west of Ayii Saranta and follow it to Profitis Ilias.

This walk explores the gentle agricultural hills behind Ayia Napa and Protaras. Prise yourself away from the golden beaches and you'll find that some modest exertion reveals a different world... of wind-powered wells, rich red soil producing a harvest of vegetables, quaint little churches, and a few stony tracks waiting to be explored.

The walk can be done in either direction, but it is easier to locate the **start at Ayia Napa**. From the centre, walk north on the PARALIMNI ROAD, and turn right just past the POLICE STATION on a rough road that leads in **10min** or less to the community SPORTS STADIUM. Turn left soon after passing this, and continue round the edge of PLAYING FIELDS. By now you should be seeing a radio transmitter mast in the middle distance. Keep heading towards it. A

Cyprus is surrounded by water but, surprisingly, fish are not plentiful. Fishing boats do operate — here's one at Cape Greco — and specialities you can expect to find in restaurants include swordfish, red mullet, octopus, and the ubiquitous squid or 'kalamares'.

Ayii Saranta

short distance from the mast, at about **35min**, the track makes a definite left turn. At this point, you should turn off right through an area of low trees and come to an open area from where there are views to Cape Greco.

To the left you should be able to pick out the dome and cross of **Ayii Saranta** (**50min**; Picnic 30). This most unusual, tiny church is set in a cave, and its only light comes from the dome on the hillside above it. Inside you will find evidence of a latter-day icon painter at work, and the familar candles.

Continue beyond Ayii Saranta for about 10 minutes, to a fork where 'Panayia' is signposted to the right; keep straight ahead for 'PROFITIS ILIAS', with the transmitter mast away to the left. At **1h05min** or less you should be getting views to the right of the imposing church of Profitis Ilias on its rocky perch, with Protaras behind it. Keep to the track, with the transmitter mast away to the left, and come to an ELECTRICITY WORKS. Turn sharp right off the main track here, and follow a faint track towards a round water tank. When asphalt comes underfoot at a villa development, keep downhill, then climb the steps to **Profitis Ilias** (**2h**). Views from the church and its pedestal are pleasing; the church is modern but very attractive inside and out. From Profitis Ilias descend steps to the main coast road and pick up a bus or taxi.

SERVICE TAXI AND BUS TIMETABLES

Below are some destinations you may wish to visit by public transport. The number after the place name is the **timetable number**. Timetables follow on the next 12 pages, but do remember to get a current timetable from a bus station or tourist information office. Departure points for buses and service taxis are shown on the town plans (see pages 8-13) and on the walking maps.

Agros — Lemesos B8
Amathus — Lemesos B9
Ayia Napa (Agia Napa)
— Larnaka C7, D1
— Lefkosia A10, A11
— Paralimni D3
Ayios Neophytos — Pafos E9
Baths of Aphrodite — Polis F1
Coral Bay — Pafos E8
Kakopetria — Lefkosia A8
Kissonerga — Pafos E7
Kiti — Larnaka C9
Kykko Monastery
— Lefkosia A13
Lachi — Polis F1
Larnaka (Larnaca)
all destinations C1-C11
— Ayia Napa C7
— Kiti C9
— Lefkosia A1, A4, C1, C4
— Lemesos B2, B6, C2, C5
— Pafos C3, E3
— Paralimni C8
— Perivolia C10
— Protaras C8
— tourist beach C11
Lefkosia (Nicosia)
all destinations A1-A13
— Ayia Napa A10, A11
— Kakopetria A8
— Kykko Monastery A13
— Larnaka A1, A4, C1, C4
— Lemesos A2, A5, A12, B1, B4
— Pafos A3, A6, E2
— Paralimni A11
— Platres A7
— Polis A12
— Protaras A11
— Troodos A9
Lemesos (Limassol)
all destinations B1-B10
— Agros B8
— Amathus B9
— Larnaka B2, B6, C2, C5
— Lefkosia A2, A5, B1, B4

— Pafos B3, B5, E1, E4
— Platres B7
— Prodhromos B7
— Yermasoyia B10
Pafos (Paphos)
all destinations E1-E9
— Ayios Neophytos E9
— Coral Bay E8
— Kissonerga E7
— Larnaka C3, E3
— Lefkosia A3, A6, A12, E2
— Lemesos B3, B5, E1, E4
— Polis E5
— Pomos E6
— Tala E9
Paralimni
— Ayia Napa D3
— Larnaka C8, D2
— Lefkosia A11
— Protaras D3
Petra tou Romiou
— Lemesos B5
— Pafos E4
Pissouri
— Lemesos B5
— Pafos E4
Platres
— Lefkosia A7
— Lemesos B7
Polis
— Baths of Aphrodite F1
— Lachi F1
— Lefkosia A12
— Pafos E5
Pomos — Pafos E6
Prodhromos
— Lefkosia A7
— Lemesos B7
Protaras
— Ayia Napa D3
— Larnaka C8
— Lefkosia A11
— Paralimni D3
Tala — Pafos E9
Troodos — Lefkosia A9
Yermasoyia — Lemesos B10

121

No	Itinerary	Company	Address or Location

Services from LEFKOSIA (Nicosia)

SERVICE TAXIS (all are operated by 'Pagkypria Eteria

A1	**Lefkosia to LARNAKA**	Cyprus Interurban-Taxi	27 Leoforos Stasinou – Municipal Parking Place
A2	**Lefkosia to LEMESOS**	*as A1 above*	*As A1 above*
A3	**Lefkosia to PAFOS**	*as A1 above*	*As A1 above*

BUS SERVICES — INTERCITY

A4	**Lefkosia to LARNAKA**	Intercity Buses	Solomos Square
A5	**Lefkosia to LEMESOS** *Two* bus companies serve this route.	Intercity Buses	Solomos Square
		Alepa Bus	Tripolis Bastion (Solomos Square)
A6	**Lefkosia to PAFOS** *Two* bus companies serve this route, both run via Lemesos.	Nea Amorza	Solomos Square
		Alepa Bus	Tripolis Bastion (Solomos Square)

BUS SERVICES — RURAL AND SUBURBAN

A7	**Lefkosia to PLATRES** (Route: Platres—Prodhromos—Pedhoulas)	Pedoulas-Platres Bus	34 Leonidou (off Omirou)
	PLATRES to Lefkosia (Route: Pedhoulas—Prodhromos—Platres)	Pedoulas-Platres Bus	for departure point enquire at tourist office
A8	**Lefkosia to KAKOPETRIA**	Clarios Bus	Station, Costanza Bastion (200m east of Eleftheria Square)
	KAKOPETRIA to Lefkosia	Clarios Bus	Kakopetria village
A9	**Lefkosia to TROODOS** ***TROODOS to Lefkosia***	Clarios Bus Clarios Bus	as A8 above Troodos main street

Telephone No	Timetable

Yperastikon Taxi' = Cyprus Interurban Taxi Co)

22-730888 27-77474	*Daily,* every half hour from 06.00 to 18.00 (19.00 Sat/Sun)
As A1 above	*As A1 above*
As A1 above	*As A1 above*

22-665814 or 22-778841	*Mon-Fri:* 09.00, 13.00, 14.30, 16.00, 17.45, 18.30 (summer only) *Sat:* 09.00, 13.00
22-665814	*Mon-Fri:* 06.00, 08.30, 10.30, 12.30, 14.30, 16.00, 17.00 *Sat:* 10.00, 14.00
29-625027	*Summer:* 14.45, 15.45 *(Mon/Tue/Thu/Fri)* 12.45 *(Wed/Sat)* *Winter:* 14.45 *(Mon/Tue/Thu/Fri)* 12.45 *(Wed/Sat)*
26-936822 or 26-936740	*Mon-Fri:* 06.30 (departs Lemesos 09.30) *Sat:* 07.00 (departs Lemesos 09.30)
26-664636	*Summer:* 15.45 *(Mon/Tue/Thu/Fri)* 12.45 *(Wed/Sat)* *Winter:* 14.45 *(Mon/Tue/Thu/Fri)* 12.45 *(Wed/Sat)*

22-952437 or 29-618865	*Mon-Sat only:* 12.15
22-952437 or 29-618865	*Mon-Sat only:* 06.00 (does not call at Platres on Saturdays unless reserved in advance)
22-753234	*Mon-Sat:* 06.10, 10.20, 11.30, 13.00, 14.00, 14.30, 15.30, 16.20, 16.45, 17.30 (18.30, 19.00 in summer) *Sun:* 08.00, 18.00 *(July and August)* *Mon-Sat:* 05.00, 05.20, 05.45, 06.10, 06.30, 08.00, 13.30, 14.30 *Sun:* 06.00, 16.30 *(July and August)*
22-753234	*Weekdays only:* 11.30 *Weekdays only:* 13.30

No	Itinerary	Company	Address or Location
A10	**Lefkosia to AYIA NAPA**	EMAN	Bus stop: Constanza Bastion (Bayractar)
	AYIA NAPA to Lefkosia	EMAN	bus station between t monastery square and the harbour
A11	**Lefkosia to PARALIMNI, PROTARAS, AYIA NAPA**	PEAL Bus	Bus stop: 'OCHI' Stat and 27 Stasinou Aver
	AYIA NAPA, PROTARAS, PARALIMNI to Lefkosia	PEAL Bus	Ag Georgios Square, in Paralimni or hotels area in Protaras
A12	**Lefkosia to POLIS** Via Lemesos and Pafos	'Solis' Mini Bus	Tripolis Bastion
	POLIS to Lefkosia Via Pafos and Lemesos	'Solis' Mini Bus	for departure point enquire at tourist offi
	Two mini-buses serve this route	'Lysos' Mini Bus	for departure point enquire at tourist offi
A13	**Lefkosia to KYKKO** **KYKKO to Lefkosia**	Kambos Bus Kambos Bus	Leonidou Street Kykko Monastery

Services from LEMESOS (Limassol)

SERVICE TAXIS (all are operated by 'Pagkypria Eteria

B1	Lemesos to LEFKOSIA	Cyprus Interurban Taxi	21 Thessalonikis St, Othelos Building or Corner Kavazoglou & Misiaouli
B2	Lemesos to LARNAKA	*as B1 above*	*as B1 above*
B3	Lemesos to PAFOS	*as B1 above*	*as B1 above*

BUS SERVICES — INTERCITY

B4	Lemesos to LEFKOSIA *Three* operators serve this route	Intercity Buses	old port/seafront road
		Nea Amorza	old port/seafront road
		Alepa Bus	Panikos Kiosk/seafron
B5	Lemesos to PAFOS *Two* operators serve this route	Alepa Bus	Panikos Kiosk/seafron
		Nea Amorza	old port/seafront road
B6	Lemesos to LARNAKA	Intercity Buses	old port/seafront road

Telephone No	Timetable
23-721321	*Mon-Sat only:* 15.00
23-721321	*Mon-Sat only:* 08.00
23-821318	*Mon-Sat only:* 13.30
23-821318 or 29-484818	*Mon-Sat only:* departs Protaras 07.00*, departs Paralimni 07.30* *seats must be booked one day in advance
22-666388	*Mon-Sat only:* 12.00
26-352332 or 29-431363	*Mon-Sat only:* 05.00 (no bus on Tuesdays)
29-414777	*Mon-Sat only:* 05.30 (no bus on Wednesdays)
not known	*Mon-Sat only:* 12.00 *Mon-Sat only:* 06.00

Yperastikon Taxi' = Cyprus Interurban Taxi Co)

25-364114	*Daily,* every half hour from 06.00 to 18.00 (19.00 Sat/Sun)
25-575823	*Daily,* every half hour from 06.00 to 18.00 (19.00 Sat/Sun)
as B1 above	*as B1 above*
as B1 above	*as B1 above*

22-665814	*Mon-Fri:* 06.00, 07.30, 09.00, 10.30, 12.30 14.30, 18.00; *Sat:* 07.00, 12.00,
26-936822	*Mon-Fri:* 16.00; *Sat:* 14.15
29-625027	*Mon/Tue/Thur/Fri:* 09.30; *Wed/Sat:* 09.00
29-625027	*Mon/Tue/Thur/Fri:* 17.00 (16.00 in winter) *Wed/Sat:* 14.00
26-936822	*Mon-Sat:* 09.30
24-643492 or 24-643493	*Mon-Fri:* 07.45, 10.00, 13.30, 16.00 *Sat:* 07.45, 10.00, 13.00

No	Itinerary	Company	Address or Location

BUS SERVICES — RURAL AND SUBURBAN

No	Itinerary	Company	Address or Location
B7	Lemesos to PLATRES	Travel Express	21 Thessalonikis (next to Othello cinema
	PLATRES to Lemesos	Travel Express	Platres centre
B8	Lemesos to AGROS	Agros Bus	corner of Irinis & Enoseos Streets
	AGROS to Lemesos	Agros Bus	Agros village centre
B9	Lemesos to AMATHUS	EAL Bus 6, 30	main bus stop, Lemesos market
	AMATHUS to Lemesos	EAL Bus 6, 30	Hotel Meridien
B10	Lemesos to YERMASOYIA	EAL Bus 10, 13	main bus stop, Lemesos market
	YERMASOYIA to Lemesos	EAL Bus 10, 13	main square in Yermasoyia

Services from LARNAKA

SERVICE TAXIS (all are operated by 'Pagkypria Eteria

C1	Larnaka to LEFKOSIA	Cyprus Interurban Taxi	Corner Papakyriakou and Marsellou or 2 Kimonos Street
C2	Larnaka to LEMESOS	*as C1 above*	*As C1 above*
C3	Larnaka to PAFOS	*as C1 above*	*As C1 above*

BUS SERVICES — INTERCITY

C4	Larnaka to LEFKOSIA	Intercity Buses	bus stop opposite the Four Lanterns Hotel
C5	Larnaka to LEMESOS	Intercity Buses	bus stop opposite the Four Lanterns Hotel

Larnaka to PAFOS — *Service via Lemesos; see Timetables C5 and*

BUS SERVICES — RURAL AND SUBURBAN

C6	Larnaka to PARALIMNI (Route: Larnaka—Paralimni—Protaras)	PEAL Bus	bus stop opposite the police station, Leoforo Archbishop Makariou

Telephone No	Timetable
25-364114	*Mon-Sat only:* 11.15
	Mon-Sat only: 07.00
	Mon-Sat: 11.50
	Mon-Sat: 07.00
	Buses 6 and 30 operate year round along the coast road; times from the tourist office
	Mon-Fri only: 08.35, 09.05, 09.30, 10.15, 10.45, 11.25, 11.55, 13.10, 15.10, 15.50, 17.05
	Mon-Fri only: 08.00, 08.30, 09.00, 09.40, 10.10, 10.50, 11.20, 12.35, 14.05, 15.15, 16.30

Yperastikon Taxi' = Cyprus Interurban Taxi Co)

Telephone No	Timetable
24-661010	*Daily,* every half hour from 06.00 to 18.00 (19.00 Saturdays and Sundays)
24-661010	*as above*
As C1 above	*As C1 above*
As C1 above	*As C1 above*
24-643492 or 24-643493	*Mon-Fri:* 06.45, 09.00, 11.00, 14.30, 16.00 *Sat:* 06.45, 09.00, 13.00
24-643492 or 24-722700	*Mon-Fri:* 08.00, 10.00, 13.00, 16.30 *Sat:* 08.00, 10.00, 13.00
23-821318	*Summer, Mon-Fri:* 08.00, 12.00, 13.45, 14.30, 16.30 *Summer, Sat:* 09.00, 12.00, 13.30, 15.00 *Winter, Mon-Fri:* 09.00, 12.00, 13.45, 14.30, 16.30 *Winter, Sat:* 11.00, 12.00, 15.00

No	Itinerary	Company	Address or Location
C7	**Larnaka to AYIA NAPA**	EMAN	bus stop opposite the Four Lanterns Hotel
	AYIA NAPA to Larnaka: *see Timetable D1*		
C8	**Larnaka to PARALIMNI and PROTARAS** (Route: Larnaka— Paralimni—Protaras)	PEAL Bus	bus stop opposite the police station, Leoforc Archbishop Makariou
	PROTARAS and PARALIMNI to Larnaka (via Deryneia and Frenaros)	PEAL Bus	Ag Georgios Square ir Paralimni, or from hotel area, Protaras
C9	**Larnaka to KITI** (Angeloktistos Church)	Larnaka Buses Ltd, Bus No 6-7	bus stop in Ayios Lazaros Square
	KITI to Larnaka	Bus No 6-7	Kiti village (Angeloktistos Church
C10	**Larnaka to PERIVOLIA**	Larnaka Buses Ltd Bus No 10	bus stop in Ayios Lazaros Square
	PERIVOLIA to Larnaka	Larnaka Buses Ltd Bus No 10	Pervolia village
C11	**Larnaka to TOURIST BEACH EAST of Larnaka**	Bus No 18 (Tourist Plage)	next to Larnaka Tourist Office
	TOURIST BEACH EAST to Larnaka	Bus No 18 (Tourist Plage)	tourist beach east of Larnaka

Services from Ayia Napa, Paralimni, Protaras

BUS SERVICES — RURAL AND SUBURBAN

D1	Ayia Napa to LARNAKA	EMAN	bus station between monastery square and the harbour
	LARNAKA to Ayia Napa: *see Timetable C7*		

Telephone No	Timetable
23-721321	*Summer, Mon-Sat:* 08.30, 09.30, 10.30, 11.30, 13.00, 14.00, 15.30, 16.30, 17.30 *Summer, Sun:* 08.30, 10.30, 13.00, 16.30 *Winter, Mon-Sat only:* 08.30, 09.30, 10.30, 13.00, 14.00, 16.30
23-821318	*Summer, Mon-Fri:* 08.00, 12.00, 13.45, 14.30, 16.30 *Summer, Sat:* 09.00, 12.00, 13.30, 15.00 *Winter, Mon-Fri:* 09.00, 12.00, 13.45, 14.30, 16.30 *Winter, Sat:* 11.00, 12.00, 15.00
23-821318	*Summer, Mon-Fri:* 09.00, 10.30, 13.30 *Sat:* 08.00, 09.00, 10.30 *Winter, Mon-Fri:* 09.30, 14.00 *Sat:* 09.00, 10.30, 13.30
24-657466	*Mon-Sat:* 06.40, 08.00, 09.00, 10.00, 11.00, 12.00, 13.05, 14.00, 15.30, 16.30, 17.00, 17.45, (19.00 in summer only) (Last bus on Saturdays: 13.05)
	Mon-Sat: 06.10, 07.00, 08.30, 09.30, 10.30, 11.30, 12.30, 13.20, 14.30, 15.40, 16.00, 17.00 (Last bus on Saturdays:12.30)
24-650477 or 29-524740	*Mon-Fri:* 07.55, 10.00, 12.00, 13.45, 16.30, 17.45; *Sat:* 08.00, 10.00, 12.00, 13.30
	Mon-Fri: 08.30, 10.30, 12.45, 15.30, 17.00; *Sat:* 08.30, 10.30, 13.00
24-652929 or 24-650477	*Mon-Fri:* every half hour from 07.30 to 18.00 *Sat:* every half hour from 08.00 to 14.00
24-652929 or 24-650477	*Mon-Fri:* every half hour from 07.30 to 18.00 *Sat:* every half hour from 08.00 to 14.00

23-721321	*Mon-Sat:* 08.00, 09.00, 10.00, 11.00*, 12.00, 14.00, 15.00*, 16.00, 17.00* *Sun:* 09.00*, 11.00*, 15.00*, 16.00* *these buses run May to October only

No	Itinerary	Company	Address or Location
D2	**Paralimni to LARNAKA**	Paralimni Bus	Ag Georgios Square, Paralimni
	LARNAKA to Paralimni: *see Timetable C8*		
D3	**Ayia Napa to PARALIMNI (via PROTARAS)**	EMAN	bus station between monastery square and the harbour
	PARALIMNI to Ayia Napa (via PROTARAS) (Route: Paralimni—Protaras — Ayia Napa—Protaras— Paralimni)	PEAL Bus	Ag Georgios Square in Paralimni or hotels area in Protaras

Services from PAFOS

SERVICE TAXIS (all are operated by 'Pagkypria Eteria

E1	**Pafos to LEMESOS**	Cyprus Interurban Taxi	8 Evagora Pallikaridis
E2	**Pafos to LEFKOSIA** — *as Timetable E1*		
E3	**Pafos to LARNAKA** — *as Timetable E1*		

BUS SERVICES — INTERCITY

E4	**Pafos to LEMESOS**	Nea Amoroza	79 Evagora Pallikaridis (north of the main squa
	Pafos to LEFKOSIA — *Service via Lemesos; see Timetables E4 and*		
	Pafos to LARNAKA — *Service via Lemesos; see Timetable E4 and*		

BUS SERVICES — RURAL AND SUBURBAN

E5	**Pafos to POLIS**	Nea Amoroza	79 Evagora Pallikaridis (north of the main squa
	POLIS to Pafos	Nea Amoroza	Polis centre

Telephone No	Timetable
23-821318	*May-Oct:* 09.00, 10.30, 13.30 *(Mon-Fri only)* 08.00, 09.00, 10.30 *(Sat only)* *Nov-Apr:* 09.30, 14.00 *(Mon-Fri only);* 09.00, 10.30, 13.30 *(Sat only)*
23-721321	*Mon-Sat:* 09.00, 09.30*, 10.00, 10.30*, 11.00, 11.30*, 12.00, 13.00, 14.00, 14.45*, 16.00, 16.30*, 17.00, 17.30*, 17.45*, 18.00*, 18.30*, 19.00*, 19.30*, 20.00* *Sun:* 09.00*, 10.00*, 11.00*, 12.00*, 13.00*, 14.00*, 16.00*, 17.00* *these buses run May to October only
23-821318	*Daily, May-Oct:* 09.00, 09.30*, 10.00, 10.30*, 11.00, 11.30*, 12.00, 13.00, 14.00, 15.00*, 16.00, 16.30*, 17.00, 17.30*, 18.00, 18.30*, 19.00, 20.00* *not on Sundays *Nov-Apr, Mon-Sat only:* 09.00, 10.00, 11.00 12.00, 13.00, 14.00, 16.00, 17.00

Yperastikon Taxi' = Cyprus Interurban Taxi Co)

26-933181	*Daily,* every half hour from 06.00 to 18.00 (19.00 Saturdays and Sundays)
26-936822	*Mon-Fri:* 14.30; *Sat:* 13.00
26-236822 or 26-936740	*Mon-Fri:* 06.20, 09.00, 10.00, 11.00, 12.00, 13.00, 14.00, 16.00, 17.00, 18.00, 19.00 (June-Sep) *Sat:* 09.00, 10.00, 11.00, 13.00, 14.30, 16.00
26-321114/5	*Mon-Fri:* 05.30, 06.30, 08.00, 10.00, 11.00, 12.00, 13.45, 14.30, 16.00, 17.00, 18.00 (summer) *Sat:* 06.30, 07.30, 10.00, 12.00, 13.15, 14.30

No	Itinerary	Company	Address or Location
E6	**Pafos to POMOS**	Nea Amoroza	79 Evagora Pallikaridis (north of the main squa
	POMOS to Pafos	Nea Amoroza	Pomos village
E7	**Pafos to KISSONERGA**	Alepa Bus	Karavella station or the market
	KISSONERGA to Pafos		Kissonerga village
E8	**Pafos to CORAL BAY** *Two* buses serve this route, both run by Alepa	Bus No 15 (Alepa Bus)	Yeroskipos Beach; stop along the coastal road
		Bus No 10 (Alepa Bus)	Karavella station or the market
	CORAL BAY to Pafos		Coral Bay
E9	**Pafos to TALA**	Alepa Bus	Karavella station or the market
	TALA to Pafos	Alepa Bus	Tala village

Services from POLIS

BUS SERVICES — RURAL AND SUBURBAN

No	Itinerary	Company	Address or Location
F1	**Polis to the BATHS OF APHRODITE and LACHI**	Nea Amoroza	Polis centre
	LACHI and the BATHS OF APHRODITE to Polis	Nea Amoroza	Latchi harbour or Tourist Pavilion at Baths of Aphrodite

Telephone No	Timetable
26-236822 or 26-936740	*Mon-Sat:* 11.00, 16.00
	Mon-Sat: 13.00
26-934410	*enquire at the Pafos Tourist Office* (not included in Cyprus Tourism timetables)
26-934410	*May-Oct:* 08.00-23.00 daily, every 15-20 min. *Nov-Apr:* 08.00-18.00 daily, every 15-20 min.
26-934410	*Mon-Sat:* 06.30-17.45, every 20 min.
	Frequency as above
26-934410	09.30, 12.00, 15.00 *(Mon-Thur)*, 15.30 *(Fri)*, 17.00 *(Mon-Fri)*
	enquire at the Pafos Tourist Office (not included in Cyprus Tourism timetables)
26-321114	*June-Oct only:* 10.00, 12.00, 15.00 *(Mon-Fri)*
26-321114	*June-Oct only:* 10.30, 12.30, 15.30 *(Mon-Fri)*

● Index

Geographical entries only are included in this index. For other entries, see Contents, page 3. A page number in *italic type* indicates a map reference, a page number in **bold type** indicates a photograph or drawing. Both of these may be in addition to a text reference on the same page. 'TM' refers to the large-scale walking map on the reverse of the touring map. Transport timetables are given on pages 121 to 133.